DATE DUE	MAR 6 '00
JUN 1 9 '00	
DEC 2 1 2003	
MAY 2 8 2004	

THE
FIBREGLASS
MANUAL

THE
FIBREGLASS
MANUAL

A practical guide to the use of glass reinforced plastics

KEITH NOAKES

Windrow & Greene

This edition published in Great Britain by
Windrow & Greene Ltd,
5 Gerrard Street,
London W1V 7LJ.

© Keith Noakes 1998

Produced for Windrow & Greene
by The Shadetree Press, East Sussex.

Printed in the UK

A CIP catalogue record for this book is available from the
British Library.

ISBN 1 85915 088 8

Contents

	Introduction	6
1	Tools & equipment	8
2	Materials	12
3	Making patterns	20
4	Making moulds	28
5	Polyester & vinylester laminating by hand	50
6	Epoxy laminating by hand	74
7	Phenolic laminating	86
8	Positive-pressure laminating with matched moulds	90
9	Spray laminating	92
10	Closed-mould laminating (RTM)	94
11	Foam as a core material	102
12	Repairs & modifications	106
13	Troubleshooting	114
14	Resin casting	118
15	Health & safety	124
	Conclusion	126
	Index	127

Introduction

Below **The ornately carved barge-boards of this house had become too rotten to renovate, except for one section that was used to produce a mould for GRP replacements. This photograph shows the latter being installed.**

Below centre **This building makes use of GRP cladding panels. Note the blackened section resulting from a fire. This was easily repaired by fitting a new panel.**

Below right **GRP is widely used in the manufacture of children's playground equipment, such as this slide.**

Glass reinforced plastic (GRP), or plain fibreglass to many people, has been around for a long time, and has been used in a very wide range of applications, among them automotive bodywork, boats and canoes, aircraft, furniture, pool liners, buildings and leisure equipment. Regardless of application, in most cases, the GRP components will have been manufactured by a specialist fibreglass company. Many of these will have been small businesses that will have learned their skills as they went along.

As with any craft, the skills needed to work with GRP can be achieved with time, and experience gained with practice. However, almost all of the applications mentioned, and the limitless possibilities not mentioned, are within the capabilities of anyone who is prepared to learn a new skill, and it is the intention of this book to provide a guide for those who wish to take advantage of the limitless potential that GRP has to offer.

I have tried to make the text as practical as possible, with dos and don'ts so that you will avoid pitfalls, and, where appropriate, I have recommended ways of keeping costs down by the use of everyday materials in moulds and patterns. Whether you want to produce a one-off component, a low number or even large numbers on a production basis, information is provided to allow you to achieve that end.

The most widely used GRP system comprises glass fibres in combi-

nation with polyester resin. This is cheap and easy to work with, and it requires the minimum of equipment. However, if your aim is to produce a very light component, or something with greater structural strength, the book also covers the use of epoxy resin systems with higher-performance fibres. While special equipment is required for these systems, and the basic materials are more expensive, the relevant techniques can still be carried out by anyone in their garage or home workshop.

Several companies and people provided invaluable help during the preparation of this book, so I would like to extend my thanks to the following: Plastech Thermoset Tectronics, Gunnislake, Cornwall; Fibrecraft, Conington, Cambs; S.J. Rolls Plastics Ltd, Brandon, Suffolk; Bridge Boatyard, Ely, Cambs; Colourex, Brandon, Suffolk; Harley Engineering, Sawtry, Cambs; MFA/Como Drills, Worth, Kent; K&C Mouldings (England) Ltd, Diss, Norfolk; M. Carpenter; G. Edens; Alan Harper; Stan Rolls; Paul Tommé; Phil Wenn; Alan Bond; and last, but not least, Roy Jackson, my very patient typist.

Keith Noakes
November 1997

Above **An unusual application for GRP was in the construction of this model Stone Age village.**

Above left **When it comes to leisure products, the uses for GRP are endless. These boats are typical examples.**

Below **The skirt and roof extension panels shown on this large truck were made from wet-lay-up GRP.**

Tools & equipment

For most normal polyester GRP applications, the tools required are simple everyday items and relatively cheap, which means that anyone wishing to utilize GRP for the first time, or to produce a one-off component or structure, will be faced with a comparatively small financial outlay. To a large degree, the actual list of tools and equipment required will depend on the complexity and size of the intended project, and the forms of pattern and mould required.

Brushes
For most GRP projects, you will need a selection of paint brushes, ranging in size from 13-75mm (½ to 3in), which will cover most applications. Very cheap brushes can be used for laminating, but it is a good idea to buy better quality examples for applying gel coats, as the cheapest brushes tend to shed their bristles, and if the component is to have a self-coloured finish, errant bristles can spoil the appearance. Many of the brushes available from GRP suppliers have light coloured bristles that don't tend to show in a glass laminate if they shed, but almost any type of brush will do.

Mixing vessels
Vessels for mixing resins will also be required and can be obtained from a GRP supplier. They usually take the form of waxed paper beakers (suitable for small resin mixes) or plastic pails or buckets (for larger mixes). As the beakers have to be purchased in batches, for a small job, it is a good idea to utilize plastic containers from the home. Empty spring water bottles or milk containers with the tops cut off make ideal mixing vessels. Most plastic household containers are resistant to polyester resin, although some very thin clear types are not, so test them first. Plastic ice cream cartons are particularly suitable for mixing larger volumes of the higher-viscosity (thicker) gel coat systems. Wooden spatulas are available for mixing, but almost anything will do; a metal spatula is best, as it can be wiped clean directly after each use.

Consolidating rollers
Particularly important items of equipment are laminating rollers, which are used to consolidate the lamination. These range in width from about 50 to 150mm (2 to 6in). The diameter of rollers can also vary, but is usually in the region of 18mm (¾in). Each laminating roller consists of a steel wire

frame with a handle, very much like a conventional paint roller. In many cases, the roller element takes the form of a metal shaft with slots running along its length, rather like an elongated gear wheel. Another form of roller consists of a series of metal discs placed on the wire frame with thin spacers between them. A simple way to make this type of roller yourself is to bend up the frame from 3mm (⅛in), or similar, steel rod or wire. Then fit it with a quantity of ordinary steel washers of the required diameter, with smaller-diameter washers in between as spacers. For general use, a roller diameter of around 18mm (¾in) will be suitable, although it can also be very useful to possess a consolidating roller of smaller diameter for working in narrow recesses.

Another roller that may be utilized is a normal mohair paint roller. In this case, it's not for laminating, but for applying gel coats to larger moulds. Whether you apply gel coats with a roller or brush will depend on your own personal preference, since both will give the desired coverage. Roller coating can be quicker, but on the other hand, brushes will be easier to clean.

Catalyst measure

Although many users of polyester resin systems add the catalyst by guesswork, since the proportions are not ultra critical, it makes sense to purchase a catalyst measure from the resin suppliers. This consists of a calibrated vessel mounted on a squeezable plastic bottle. You simply hold it upright and squeeze the bottle to fill the measure with the required amount of catalyst. When you release pressure on the bottle, the catalyst remains in the vessel ready to be poured into the resin. For large volumes, it is a good idea to use an electronic balance of some type to weigh out the required amount of catalyst.

Essential extras

You need a good craft knife, or better still, two—one purely for cutting glass cloth, and the other for general use during laminating. Other essentials include a range of abrasive papers: some very coarse for trimming

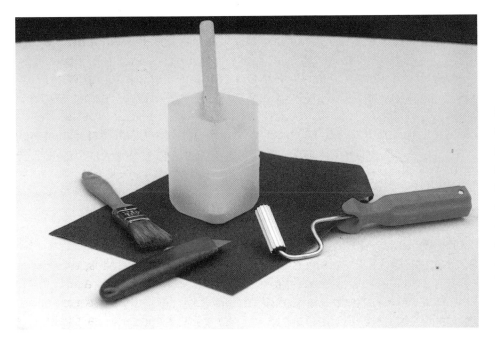

Shown here is the minimum amount of equipment needed to make simple GRP components: a mixing vessel (in this case a cut-down milk carton), a wooden stirring spatula, a craft knife, a paint brush, abrasive material and a consolidating roller. Some small components can be made without a roller, but the task will be easier, and the result better, if one is used.

The addition of a catalyst measuring bottle, electric sander, a range of brush sizes and various grades of abrasive sheets results in an equipment collection that will cope with a wide variety of GRP applications. Other tools can be added when needed.

finished laminates, and some very fine for finishing. An electric angle grinder or sander will be an enormous help when trimming laminates, especially where they are quite thick, such as on moulds. The same goes for an electric drill. Although a hand drill will cope with most drilling jobs, an electric drill will be easier and quicker to use, and it can also be fitted with a mop for polishing moulds or finished components.

When the use of multi-section moulds is envisaged, spanners will be required for the bolts that hold them together. If you don't already possess a selection of spanners for working on your car, two adjustable spanners will handle most jobs.

You will also need a rubber mallet and a Surform or similar type of plane for use when making shaped patterns. The pattern materials will vary, so a coarse type of abrasive plane is preferable to a blade type. G-cramps will be very useful, but they are not essential, especially where the component to be made is likely to be small or a one-off.

Other requirements include rubber gloves and overalls. Disposable paper overalls are best, as washing resin impregnated clothing is difficult. Protective spectacles must be worn when trimming laminates, while dust masks are very desirable.

Special requirements

More equipment is required for GRP constructions based on epoxy resin systems, but the methods and any specific equipment will be outlined in the respective chapter. Whatever type of laminating is to be carried out, basic safety items that should always be at hand include a first aid kit and a suitable hand cleaner, the latter being available from most GRP materials suppliers.

Established GRP workshops will have an extensive range of tools and aids, many of which will have been designed to speed up the processing of components for purely commercial reasons, although many jobs could be completed with fewer facilities. Therefore, it is not possible to give a

The basic protective clothing for GRP work: overalls (in this case, disposable); safety goggles and disposable dust mask used when trimming or sanding laminates; rubber gloves when using resins; and industrial gloves to handle sharp-edged laminates when removing them from moulds or trimming.

finite list of tools and equipment, as the requirements will depend on the user and the job in hand. It is best to make a start with the essentials and to purchase other tools or equipment as required. Common sense will prevail in many cases, and often it will be possible to complete a project with tools that are already to hand. After all, in the main, GRP work is a manual craft dependent more upon the skill of the practitioner than the wide range of available equipment. Once the basics have been explained, most GRP users develop their own variations of the standard techniques, employing tools and materials that suit their methods.

2

Materials

It would be impossible to list all the products available to those wishing to utilize GRP technology, as there are so many variants of the basic materials, with individual manufacturers supplying their own particular versions. In addition, there are endless specialized materials for specific jobs. Thus, the materials described here are the most commonly used for a very wide range of GRP applications, both by professionals and amateurs.

Resins and gel coats

Polyester laminating resins are available virtually world-wide, and are usually obtainable in small and large quantities. There will be differences from one manufacturer to another, and differing qualities; some suppliers offer very cheap resins. Modified resins may also be encountered. For example, some may have fire-retardant properties, or improved heat resistance, or better resistance to constant water exposure.

However, choosing the correct resin is not as difficult as it might seem to the first-time user. General-purpose polyester resin systems will be suitable for most automotive applications, non-structural aircraft parts, and for most boat use, as well as the long list of general applications.

When determining the resin to use, the gel coat type should be considered at the same time. The reason for this is that for some special applications, the gel coat, which forms the component's outer or finished surface, will play a major part in the technical performance of the laminate.

The range of gel coats offered is likely to be narrower than for laminating resins, but there will be general-purpose types and, as with resins, modified versions with enhanced technical performance: for example, improved weathering, or heat or chemical resistance. Some gel coats produce a very hard surface, ideal for tooling, while others give a more flexible finished surface, which minimizes cracking in components that are likely to experience surface flexing in service. Some boat and large vessel builders employ flexible gel coats, but general-purpose gel coats are still the most widely used. Gel coats are available in differing viscosities (thicknesses), making them suitable for brush, roller or spray application.

Another component of the GRP laminating system that offers several choices is the catalyst, each type being formulated to make the resin mix more suitable for the desired project. For beginners, however, the basic choice of catalyst lies between high-, medium- and low-activity versions. In basic terms, the activity level controls the rate of cure. Although the percentage of catalyst in each resin mix will affect the cure time, there will be a recommended maximum and minimum amount of catalyst for each type of resin/catalyst combination. The differing activity levels enable the user to keep the combination within the recommended ratio, but to reduce the cure time of simple or small components, or ensure a quick turn-round, and to increase the cure time for large or complex components. Low-activity catalysts are also used where the lamination is to be very thick and it is essential to prevent an exotherm (the overheating of the lamination when the normal heat generated during the cure runs out of control). There are varying degrees of exotherm, but they can be extreme enough to degrade the laminate completely.

In addition to the different types of polyester resin, there is a range of vinylesters which, in general terms, are processed by very similar techniques, with the exception of the need to add an accelerator to the resin and catalyst mix. The resultant cured laminate will offer improved performance in some areas. For example, vinylesters tend to be tougher, which renders them particularly suitable for making laminated moulds, especially when these are intended to be used extensively or to have a long life.

Epoxy resins are also utilized in GRP laminating, but the processing of these is totally different to polyester resins. In most cases, epoxy resin systems require pressure to be applied throughout the cure cycle. With flat laminates, this pressure can be provided by some form of clamping arrangement, or simply by adding weights, but these methods can make it difficult to achieve consistent results or even laminates on anything other than small areas. Some flat epoxy-based laminates are made without pressure, but adequate consolidation is difficult to obtain.

The normal method of processing epoxy resins at ambient temperature is to use vacuum to apply pressure during the cure. Epoxy resins can also be force cured at elevated temperatures, but in addition to a vacuum pump, this calls for a temperature controlled oven, or autoclave. The technique requires costly equipment and falls outside the scope of this book.

Epoxy resin laminating at ambient temperature with the use of a small vacuum pump results in a tough laminate and, due to the chemical cross linking of the cured system, offers long-term stability. These properties allow the production of lightweight components through the use of woven fabrics, and the outcome can be much thinner laminates. Another major advantage is the potential offered by epoxy resin laminating in the manufacture of structural components.

A material that will almost certainly be utilized by most laminators is colouring paste, which allows the user to produce components finished to the required colour direct from the mould. The paste is simply added to the gel coat before coating the mould, and where a large volume of gel coat is likely to be used, many suppliers will offer this ready coloured to the customer's requirements. When producing large numbers of components, such pre-mixed gel coats give excellent colour continuity.

Most suppliers will also carry flow coating, or top coating, resins. These are used to coat the reverse face of an item, sealing the rough laminated surface and covering the glass fibres. The result is a smoother than normal finish that makes the laminate easier to clean in such applications as car bodies, where oil or road grime may cling to the inside.

Many laminators make their own flow coat by mixing normal laminating resin with gel coat resin. The advantage of this technique is that by mixing a high-viscosity (thick) material with a low-viscosity (thin) material, the user can produce a mix that suits spray or brush application.

Various types of casting resin are also available. Some can be used for tooling or mould making when the components are of a suitable shape, that is shallow forms, or are small. Where casting resins are used for moulds, additives can be employed to make them tougher (hard, but not brittle) and less likely to chip during use. Materials such as slate powder and marble powder are used. Most suppliers will have these, or something similar, and will recommend the ratio of powder to resin for the type they stock. The grade and type affects this ratio.

In addition to tooling and moulds, casting resins can be utilized to cast components for a wide range of engineering applications. Moreover, many electrical components can be encapsulated in resin.

Additives

A range of additives is available to make the resins suitable for a variety of applications. Among those widely employed is Aerosil. This is used to make any resin thixotropic, that is thin enough to be applied as a coating by almost any method, but with sufficient thickness to prevent running when applied thickly. Aluminium powder is added to resin systems to enhance their heat resistance and, together with copper, bronze, brass and iron powders, will give the finished item a metallic look, such as might be required for a reproduction bronze statue. When the cast item is polished, it will have the appearance of burnished metal.

Other basic fillers include china clay and talc. These materials are added to resin to produce a filler paste, which may be used in the same manner as normal automotive body filler, or for any area of GRP work where repairs are needed or where a bracket or similar item needs adding to a laminated component.

Wax is another additive mixed with polyester resin, being used to give a tack-free cured surface. In most cases, it is added to flow and top coats. Some resins contain wax to alter their laminating characteristics, but it isn't possible to go into detail on this, as individual manufacturers have their own blends, and the supplier will furnish the relevant details.

Styrene is also available as an additive. Although all polyester resins contain styrene, sometimes extra is added to reduce the viscosity of the resin or to assist the action of other additives, such as ultra-violet-resistant compounds or fire-retardant materials. However, the addition of styrene is not necessary for most normal polyester applications. Where special technical qualities are required, such as ultra-violet resistance, low smoke emission or fire-retardant properties, most suppliers can offer a suitable ready-blended resin to do the job.

Mould making materials

One item all laminators seem to make use of is modelling clay, such as Plasticene. This is employed to seal moulds and correct minor mould damage, and to remove undercuts, etc, when making patterns.

A material utilized by many laminators, especially for mould making, is two-part pourable rubber compound. In most cases, this will be silicone rubber. The material is employed to make moulds that incorporate intricate details or have pronounced undercuts. This technique is commonly utilized for moulds used for casting complex shapes, such as statues.

Most silicone moulding compounds come as pourable liquids with separate catalysts. Additives are available that make the rubber thixotropic so that it can be applied by spatula if necessary. The advantages of rubber moulds are that they can have a long life and there is no need for any form of release agent. In some cases, the shape, or more usually the size, of a rubber mould will require it to be backed up with a glass lamination to prevent mould distortion when casting or laminating the component.

Release agents

No list of laminating materials would be complete without release agents. These materials are used to ensure that the cured lamination separates cleanly from the mould or pattern. There are many variations of release agent, some of which are specific manufacturer's blends. Liquid versions are available for general-purpose use, while other types have enhanced temperature resistance, allowing them to be employed when the lamination is to be cured at elevated temperature.

The most widely used release agents, and the most simple, are waxes, some of which are formulated specifically as mould or laminate releasers. The most commonly used type for general laminating comes in solid form. Liquid waxes are also available for general-purpose use, and there are modified versions of these that have higher temperature resistance. Some laminators use high-quality car wax in solid form, but a word of warning is needed here: if you intend using automotive or some other commercial wax as a release agent, do not choose anything containing silicones. Although such waxes will release well, the silicones will migrate to the surface of the moulded component and will be very difficult to remove, causing problems if it is to be painted.

In addition to liquids and waxes, chemical release agents may be encountered in aerosol form. These do have many users, but in general, especially for those new to the technology, wax releasers are simple to use and very reliable. Such qualities are particularly important if the mould is old or the surface not exactly perfect. The wax types work well on most imperfect surfaces, although it must be said that aerosol spray release agents are useful when applied to surfaces other than fibreglass, such as a metal mould or where metal plates are incorporated in the mould, or when plugs have to be removed from the finished laminated component.

One point about wax release agents is that, with continual use, they can have a tendency to build up on the mould surface. This layer of wax can be removed with a cutting polish, although most suppliers will offer solutions for removing wax build-up.

A popular release material, used in conjunction with wax, is PVA (poly vinyl alcohol). This is water soluble and forms a thin membrane that virtually guarantees release. Some versions are blended with a solvent to speed up the drying time. The membrane produced by PVA is thin and fragile, so it must be treated carefully during the laminating process.

Liquid sealers are also available to the prospective laminator. They are needed to seal the surface of porous materials, such as wood, plaster and synthetic fillers, used for pattern making.

Although waxes are available as release agents, others will be encountered in solid form, that is as a range of sheets of differing thickness

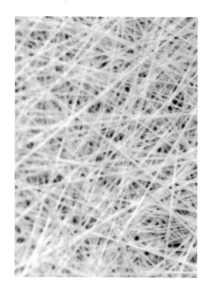

Chopped strand matt is commonly used in GRP work. Note the random arrangement of the fibres, which are held together by a dissolvable binder.

and a selection of extruded shapes, such as half-round, convex-radius, rounds and squares. In the main, these are utilized during pattern making. The extruded shapes are employed to form radii in corners, etc. Other shapes are used to make recess forms, slots, joggles and so on. Sheet wax has many uses, including making temporary changes to a mould or even small one-off moulds, but one very important application for wax sheet is when a double-sided mould is required. The method is to make a single-sided mould from a simple pattern, then a wax sheet of the same thickness as the intended laminate is formed into the mould to represent the component. The second half of the mould is laminated on to the wax. After the two halves of the mould have been separated and the wax removed, a cavity of the correct width will be left between the two sections of mould when they are reassembled. These wax sheets and forms need only to be warmed to render them mouldable or formable.

Glass reinforcements

A major consideration in all GRP components or moulds is the carrier, or reinforcement. This comes in many types, the glass fibres being offered in forms that make them suitable for a variety of applications and methods of manufacture. Therefore, it is important to select the correct form of glass fibre for the intended project, bearing in mind the ease of use and the desired mechanical performance from the finished item.

The most widely used glass fibre for general-purpose laminating is chopped strand matt. In this form, the fibres are cut into random lengths and pressed into a matt, or sheet, using some form of binder solution or powder to keep it together. It is available in differing thicknesses, and is normally sold by the ratio of its weight to surface area. The weight is usually quoted in grams per square metre or ounces per square foot, and the most widely used are 300g/1oz, 450g/1½oz, 600g/2oz and 900g/3oz.

Chopped strand matt is quite manageable, in that it can be cut to size or shape with a craft knife, then transferred to the mould for laminating. The advantage of chopped strand matt is that it is very drapable, and during lamination it forms to the mould very well. This is due to the resin dissolving the binder and freeing the short fibres so that they can follow the contours of the mould. Mechanical performance is determined by the number of layers, or plies, used.

Also widely employed by GRP laminators is glass tissue. This is very light, random-fibre glass matt. It comes in several versions, some developed to be easily moulded, and others more suitable for large flat areas.

Tissue is excellent where there is sharp detail in the mould, or where there are sharp corners or deep recesses. Being very thin and light, it forms very easily. It is common to use one or two plies in these areas prior to laminating the main glass matt. Many laminators also add a ply of tissue over the main laminate in difficult areas, as it tends to hold the matt in place until cured.

Tissue can be used for laminating very small or very detailed items. Another use is in mould making, where one or two plies of tissue can be laminated over the pattern prior to laminating the mould. Using tissue in this way will prevent surface faults, such as blow-outs (blisters) or porosity, the very fine material forming closely to the pattern's surface. It also prevents the fibres of the laminate from showing through the surface.

Other glass-fibre reinforcements include woven rovings. These consist of bundles of glass fibres woven into a matt. Since they have continuous fibres running through the matt, their use results in a higher mechanical performance from the subsequent laminate. In other words, a laminate of a specified weight will have greater stiffness and fracture strength if made from woven roving than chopped strand matt.

Woven rovings are more difficult to use because the continuous fibres offer greater resistance to being moulded, especially in tight corners and complex shapes. Therefore, serious consideration must be given to their use. However, when weight is of prime importance, or thickness is critical, woven rovings enable the required performance or thickness to be achieved using less material. Woven rovings are made in different weights, which control the thickness. Typical weights per square metre/square foot are 280g/0.9oz, 600g/2oz and 900g/3oz.

Where woven rovings are used in large components, boat or ship hulls for example, and the resultant laminate is to be very thick (10-25mm/⅜-1in or more), the interlaminar strength is very important, that is the quality of bond between each ply of the laminate. To optimize this interlaminar strength, a range of combination reinforcements is available. These take the form of woven roving with a backing of chopped strand matt. The latter may be either stitched or chemically bonded to the woven roving. The same interlaminar enhancement can be achieved by using a ply of normal chopped strand matt between each pair of woven roving plies.

Glass rovings are available in a random-fibre state, cut to a length that is suitable for spray laminating. In the main, this method is used on large components, where it is far quicker to spray the resin and fibres into the mould than use hand lay-up techniques. Spray laminating is rather messy and is practical only for a few applications. Moreover, the equipment required is expensive and would need using often to be cost effective.

Continuous glass rovings are available on spools, which are used for filament winding. This is a method of winding continuous glass fibre in conjunction with the resin. It is used to produce fibreglass pipes or tubes, or hollow components such as pressure vessels. The continuous, wound glass fibres produce a component with excellent hoop strength, that is crush or expansion resistance. The process requires special equipment that automatically controls fibre direction, which is angled to maximize performance. However, small simple jobs can be carried out with a hand wound jig that simply turns a mandrel. Note, however, that pressure vessels should only be made by those with relevant experience and the required safety clearance.

There are many other woven glass-fibre fabrics that can be utilized for polyester laminating. Among the different weave types is satin weave, a good all-round weave suitable for high performance or very high impact strength. But like most glass fabrics, the matt is held together by the pattern of the weave itself, and there is no binder to be dissolved by the resin during laminating, which means that it is much more difficult to make the woven reinforcement stay in place on corners, recesses, joggles, etc. Where the mould is of a comparatively simple form, with few or no shape changes, the use of woven fabrics becomes more practical.

Another very popular weave type is twill weave. This is easily identified by its herring-bone pattern. The nature of the weave style makes it

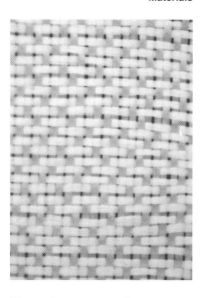

Shown here are continuous glass fibres in woven glass fabric, in this case plain weave.

very drapable, that is it is more readily formed into or over complex shapes. A point to remember about this type of weave is that more fibres run in one direction than the other, so where stiffness is a consideration, the component should be laid up with the fibre pattern orientated to take advantage of this feature. Where there are several plies, the weave pattern, or fibre direction, of each ply must be rotated to give the same number of fibres running in each direction. To achieve this, the number of plies must be taken into account. Balancing the fibres in the laminate with this type of weave is necessary to prevent warping or distortion of the finished component, which can occur with an unbalanced laminate.

One of the most widely used woven glass fabrics is plain weave. This has the same number of fibres running along its length as it does across its width (warp and weft). Since plain weave has very little fibre distortion caused by the weaving process, it produces a stiffer laminate than many other weaves, but because the fibres in this fabric are straighter than other weaves, it is more difficult to form over or into complex mould shapes. Not only does it produce a stiff laminate, but also the same number of fibres running in both directions makes it easy to keep the laminate balanced. Plain weave is ideal for large simple shapes or flat components.

When ultimate stiffness is required from the proposed laminate, or where a particular component needs stiffening in strategic areas, unidirectional fibres are used. Because the fibres are not distorted by weaving, the maximum stiffness for a set weight of glass fibre is achieved.

In most cases, unidirectional fibres are held together by fine stitching to render them manageable. It is important to remember that as there are no fibres running across the matt, there will be no strength in that direction. Where unidirectional fibres are used on their own, the plies of the laminate must be rotated in relation to each other so that the fibres run in different directions. In some cases unidirectional fibres are used in addition to woven glass fabrics to add stiffness in specific areas.

Glass-fibre tapes are available in both woven and unidirectional forms. The woven tape is useful for overlapping joints when a component is made in more than one piece and joined together as a second stage, while the unidirectional tape is mainly used to add stiffness as described.

One other glass-based material found in GRP work comprises glass flakes. These are used in resin coatings and surfaces to enhance corrosion resistance, vapour impermeability and generally improve the toughness of the selected resin system.

Core materials

Some fibreglass constructions need to be particularly stiff, especially if the structure is large. In this situation, core materials are employed. Normally, two laminated skins are separated by a central core, the resultant sandwich structure having excellent stiffness and light weight. Core materials are widely used for components with a large area, such as boat hulls and vehicle bodywork, and where large flat fibreglass panels are required.

Polyurethane foam, in solid form, is commonly chosen as a core material. It is sold in various thicknesses, usually from 6 to 50mm (¼ to 2in), and in most cases, panel sizes measure 2.4 by 1.2m (8 by 4ft) or smaller. Some suppliers offer this type of foam board faced with a glass tissue, which ensures an excellent bond with the outer laminated skins. Foams

Core materials utilized in GRP work. From left to right: paper rope, thick porous matt used to bulk the thickness of large moulds, foam and honeycomb. Many types of foam are used as cores. In some cases, end-grain balsa wood is employed.

are sold in different densities: the higher the density, the greater the compressive strength of the panel, but also the greater the weight.

Other foam types are also available, such as PVC (poly vinyl chloride) and polystyrene. However, many foams will be attacked by polyester resin, so always check with the supplier on the suitability of a particular foam for laminating with polyester resin.

Where a laminated component requires extremely high compressive strength, the core can be made from end-grain balsa wood. Although balsa appears soft, when panels are cut so that the grain runs through the thickness and not along its length, the result is a light sandwich structure with high compressive performance. Balsa is sold in a range of densities, which affects both weight and compressive performance. Some suppliers offer panels with narrow slots machined across them, making it possible to bend the material for use in a curved sandwich construction.

One of the most widely used core types is a very porous material, rather like thick blotting paper. Usually this comes in a range of thicknesses, from 1 to 5mm (1/25 to 1/5in). Many suppliers have their own name for this material, but 'core matt' is the generic term.

Core matt is not suitable for producing a lightweight sandwich structure, as it becomes saturated with resin in use and, therefore, heavy. Its most common application is to bulk up the thickness of laminated moulds and to add stiffness to large components where weight is not critical. It helps achieve the required performance from the laminate while reducing the amount of glass fabric used, providing savings in material and time because of the need for fewer plies.

Another core material is paper rope, which is sold in different thicknesses and used to form stiffening ribs in moulds and large components. When the desired number of normal plies has been laid in place, lengths of paper rope are laminated over the top to form the ribs.

Honeycomb core materials are also available, but tend to come from specialist suppliers and are not often used by polyester laminators. In the main, honeycombs may be made from aluminium, Nomex or paper and comprise panels of hexagonal cells, just like bees make. Various panel thicknesses are available.

Aluminium and Nomex are high-performance, lightweight core materials, normally used in conjunction with epoxy resin systems. Paper is a cheap honeycomb that can be utilized where the proposed panel requires a thickness that would be prohibitive in straight laminations. It tends to be used for large panels such as vehicle sides and building partitions.

3

Making patterns

True pattern making is a highly skilled profession, and it is not within the scope of this book to describe all the skills and techniques that are used. In many cases, very expensive equipment would be required and the operator (a skilled pattern maker) would need to be capable of reading and understanding the most complicated engineering drawings. That said, many patterns are made by GRP laminators, and are well within the scope of anyone wishing to carry out this stage of a project, provided the shape of the proposed component can be achieved with the tools and materials available, and the dimensional tolerances can be met. The pattern controls the quality of the finished component, as a poor pattern usually results in a poor mould, and the mould quality will be reflected in the quality of the finished component.

Amateurs who want to make patterns will need to rely on a large amount of common sense, as there is no set way of achieving the shape from which a mould will be taken. The main task when making a pattern is to find materials that can be readily formed to the required shape with a surface that can be prepared to accept release agents, and that are not likely to be attacked by the resins used to make the mould. If it is necessary to use a material that may be attacked by the resin, it is essential to seal the surface with something that is resin resistant, such as paint. In this respect, most aerosol car paints work very well as pattern surfacers.

When deciding on the materials and the method for making a pattern, size has a significant part to play. If the proposed component is a copy of an existing item (for example part of a car's bodywork, a motorcycle fairing or something similar) and an example is available, a large amount of the pattern work is already complete. However, the existing piece will have to be mounted and prepared so that a mould can be taken from it.

One important point when preparing any pattern, and especially when using an existing component, is to ensure good stability, that is the pattern must be rigid. If a pattern is flexible in any way, there is a chance that it will distort during lamination of the mould, which then will have the incorrect shape. When the subsequent moulded component is to be fitted to something else like a car body, the slightest distortion will render both component and mould useless.

Therefore, when an existing component is being used as a pattern, it must be stabilized by temporarily bonding in some form of bracing. First you must be certain that the component is of the correct shape to start with, having no distortion due to any previous damage. If you have no choice but to use a damaged component to produce a mould for replacement parts, make sure that no distortion is caused by any temporary repair carried out prior to taking a mould from it.

When repairing a damaged part to make a mould pattern, the normal procedure is first to lightly brace the back or edges. Wood is ideal for this purpose, as it can be easily shaped. Where possible, check the braced part for fit prior to mounting it for the mould making process.

When you are happy that the part is held in its correct shape, increase the amount of bracing to make it as rigid as possible. To this end, brace from one side to the other in different directions. An excellent method of attaching the bracing is to use ordinary quick setting car body filler. This can also be used to make local repairs or stiffen the part.

Attaching weirs

When the component is ready for mounting, the weirs, or dams, must be attached. These narrow rigid strips are added to the pattern around its periphery and, where necessary, around any openings, etc. Their purpose is to form a run-off to the mould. They are usually fitted so that they are perpendicular to the surface of the pattern, although sometimes on curved edges this angle will vary. Weirs are also used to form the mating faces of the mould when it is made in more than one piece. Compound shapes sometimes make multi-section moulds necessary to allow the finished product to be removed from the mould.

A wide range of materials can be used to form weirs. For components or patterns that have an undulating or shaped edge, the material must be flexible enough to follow the undulations. Thin plywood, of 1-1.5mm (⅟₃₂-⅟₁₆in) thickness, is often used, but since wood is porous, it must be treated well with wood sealer or several coats of paint. This sealing process can be avoided if you can find a suitable plastic material, such as thin ABS sheet. Most plastics of this nature are virtually self-releasing, which reduces the amount of preparation time, although it is always advisable to give the weir a coat of wax to make sure. Another material that is very good for making weirs is melamine sheet, the material used to surface kitchen worktops, which is quite flexible when not bonded to a board. These are merely suggestions, but any material that will follow the edge

A good example of a pattern. The material is laminated mahogany, which has been sealed, waxed and given a coat of PVA release agent prior to laminating the mould. This example is for the front aerofoil of a race car.

PREPARED & MOUNTED PATTERNS

A Simple pattern on rigid base.
B Simple pattern with flexible weir due to pattern shape.
C Compound-shaped pattern with central weir for split two-piece mould.
D Compound-shaped pattern, weired for three-piece mould.

In some cases, rigid base boards must be separated from the pattern to allow removal of the finished mould. When weirs are used, they should be removed after the first half of the mould has been laminated. The resulting mould flange should be treated with release agent, and the second portion of the mould laminated up to it, forming the mould split line. Flexible weirs must be rigid enough to withstand lamination.

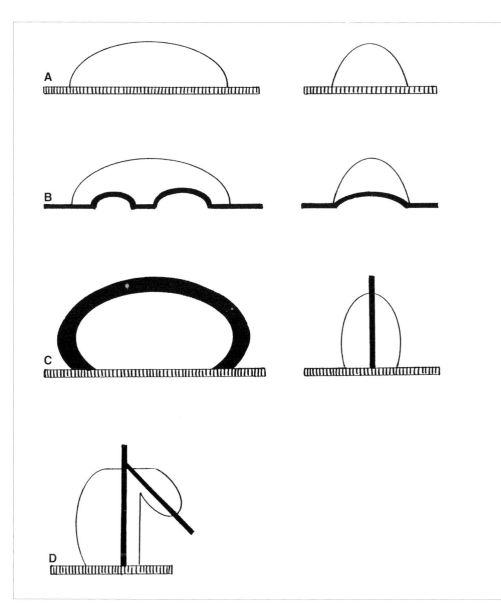

of the pattern can be used. The important requirement is to seal a porous material so that the laminated mould can be released from the pattern and the weirs.

There are various methods for attaching the weirs to the pattern. One excellent technique is to use a hot-melt glue gun. This is a small electrically operated gun that takes sticks of plastic glue. When the trigger is pulled, it pushes the glue stick through a heated nozzle to produce a bead of molten plastic that can be fed into place with the gun. This method is useful in that it is quick, the glue setting on cooling, which is quite rapid. The advantage is that you can hold a piece of weir material in place with one hand and glue it to the pattern with the other. Then you need hold the weir in place for a short time only until the glue sets.

Another useful feature of hot-melt plastic glue is that it seldom forms an unbondable joint, which means that when an existing component is to be used as a pattern, then put back into service, the weirs are easy to remove without damaging the component. Even if a good adhesive bond was made, the plastic glue is quite soft and can be cut or scraped off.

Contact adhesive can also be used for attaching weirs, provided the contact area is large enough. Otherwise this type of adhesive may not be

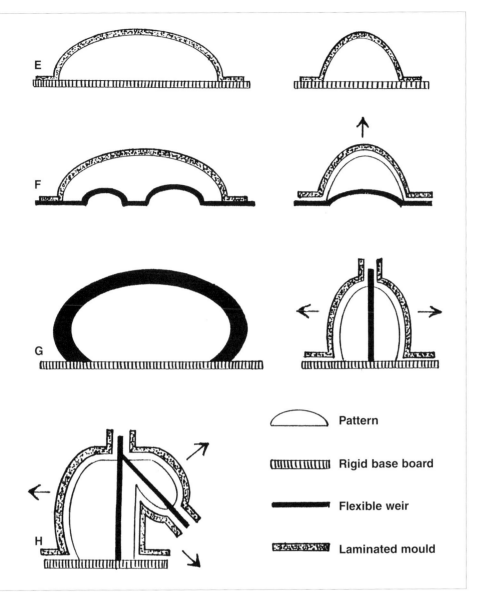

MOULD TYPES
E One-piece laminated mould.
F One-piece laminated mould.
G Split two-piece mould.
H Split three-piece mould.

Pattern

Rigid base board

Flexible weir

Laminated mould

sufficiently rigid. Plaster of Paris, or similar, can also be used, but its comparatively slow setting time can be a disadvantage, as the weirs will have to be held in place while it sets, and if the pattern is a complex shape clamping may be difficult. Automotive body filler is widely used for attaching weirs to patterns and is readily available from most accessory stores. It sets fairly quickly and is very rigid. Another advantage is that it can be used to form part of the weir itself in any areas where the pattern's shape makes it difficult to attach a sheet material. Two points to remember about using body filler, however, are that it usually has very good adhesive qualities, making it more difficult to remove if you need to, and it is porous when set, so it will require sealing if it forms any part of the weir itself.

There are no fixed rules about the attachment of weirs to patterns. Any method that holds the weirs in place while the mould is laminated will be suitable. However, when choosing a method of attachment, it must be remembered that where a split or sectional mould is planned, some of the weirs will be attached to the pattern's surface to form the mould separation points, and will need to be removed without damaging the surface.

If the pattern has a flat peripheral shape, it can simply be stuck to a flat board of some type. A melamine-faced board would be ideal because the

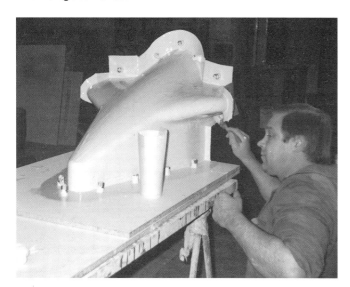

Above

This pattern is being given a gel coat as the first stage in making a mould. Note the locating devices attached to the weirs, which will be laminated into the mould flanges.

Above right

The pattern for a domestic shower tray. It has been made from a non-porous material, so light waxing will be sufficient as a release. In this case, the resulting mould will be of the male form.

melamine is almost self-releasing. Any type of stiff flat board would be suitable, however; just remember that porous materials need sealing.

Patterns from scratch

When the pattern is not based on an existing item and has to be made from scratch, there are several points to consider. The first of these is the shape of the intended component. If it is comparatively shallow, the pattern can be made from a solid material, and there are several options in this respect. Hard wood is commonly used. Some types, such as jelutong, are sold specifically for pattern making and have a very short grain structure. This enables them to be cut or machined equally in all directions to leave a smooth dense surface. These types of wood are not always easy to obtain, however, and are expensive.

Fibre board is an excellent pattern material. Consisting of wood dust bound together with resin, it is a timber-like material, but devoid of any grain structure. It is easy to profile or shape with hand or electric tools, but it does need sealing well, as it is very porous.

Specially made synthetic tooling blanks are also available. Some may be produced from filled epoxy or phenolic resin cast into blocks. These synthetic materials are claimed to be very stable, that is they maintain their shape during and after machining. They are also said to have better thermal stability than most conventional materials used for pattern making. In many cases, this last point is not that important, unless extremely close dimensional tolerances are sought.

Some types of plaster can be used for pattern making, although normally only small patterns. One problem that can occur from using plaster is shrinkage when the pattern is formed in the wet state. Also, plaster is very porous and requires extremely good sealing.

Having selected the material for a solid pattern, your next thought should be whether it can be obtained in a size that is big enough for the job. If not, sections can simply be glued together to form a larger block. This process can be useful, as the sections can be of different sizes and built up in an angular fashion to represent the proposed pattern shape, reducing the time and effort needed to achieve the final form.

The way in which the block of material is shaped will depend on the tools and equipment available. Many professional pattern makers use automatic computer controlled machines. Others, however, use a variety of hand tools, and some electric equipment, such as routers and sanders. Anyone wishing to prepare their own pattern can use whatever facilities they have to hand, or are prepared to acquire for the purpose. Obviously, an extensive range of equipment will make shaping a pattern easy, but a collection of simple tools and more personal effort can be just as effective.

In the main, whether or not a solid pattern is practical will be dictated by its size and, therefore, its weight. It is common practice to build large patterns in sections. Some are constructed as a series of boxes of varying size, joined together to make an angular structure as near to the shape of the proposed pattern as possible. Then this structure is clad in a material that can be shaped to the required form. The cladding can be fibre board, solid foam or any material that is easily shaped, again remembering that the surface will need to be sealed well. Where foam is used, it is normal to cover the rough shape with plaster or body filler. This enables a smooth accurate shape to be obtained and prevents the foam from being attacked by the resin used to make the mould.

Another popular means of building up a pattern is to cut a series of formers to the pattern profile, then join them together with spacers, or mount them on spars, rather like the skeletal framework of a model aircraft. The spaces between the formers are filled with foam or synthetic blocks, which are then shaped to the same contours as the formers.

The great advantage of this method is that the formers can be cut to an accurate profile and, when correctly spaced, produce a frame that has the correct shape in all planes. Then it is easy to finish the infill material to the frame's shape. Finally, all that is required is a thin skin of filler that can be sanded to the required finish. A good surface filler for this purpose can be made by mixing a powder filler into normal gel coat. Talc is a good example, as is china clay. Most GRP materials suppliers will have something suitable.

Regardless of the filler powder chosen, it is added to the gel coat and mixed by hand until an acceptable working consistency is reached: it must be sufficiently viscous, or thick, to resist sagging when applied. This type of home-made filler can be used fairly thickly, the powder additive making it more stable. However, where the filler is likely to be more than 6mm (¼in) thick, it is advisable to obtain the required depth by applying several

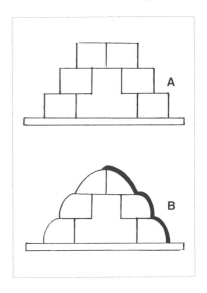

PATTERNS FROM BLOCKS
A The basic shape of the intended pattern built up in blocks. Foam is often used, but any other suitable material can be employed in the same way.
B Here the blocks have been shaped and one side of the pattern has received a layer of filler, which has been sanded to the final shape.

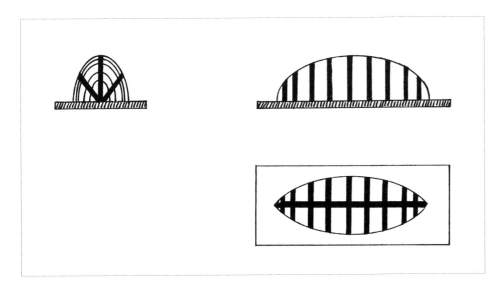

Front, side and plan elevations of a pattern made from pre-cut formers and assembled into a skeleton. The spaces between are filled with foam or some other material. In a very large pattern, the foam needs only to fill the outer portions of the gaps between the formers. The advantage of this method of pattern making is that the formers control the overall shape as the foam is sanded back to meet them in all planes.

Examples of detailed patterns prior to laminating the moulds.

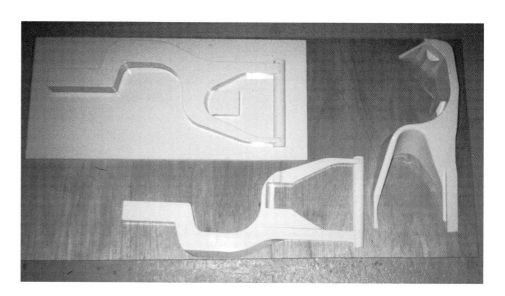

thinner layers, allowing each to cure before applying the next. This will help to prevent shrinkage and cracking.

Final shaping and finishing

When the filler is completely set, the final shaping of the pattern can be carried out. This can be done with an electric sander, or by hand with an abrasive type of shaping plane (such as a Surform) or coarse files. Final finishing should be by hand, using progressively finer grades of abrasive paper. The wet-or-dry type is commonly employed for this, the coarser grades often being used dry, followed by the finer grades used wet to achieve the best surface finish.

To some extent, the degree of finish on the pattern will depend on the surface finish required for the moulded component. There is no point in aiming to achieve a gloss finish on the pattern if the final component needs a matt surface for painting. That said, it is very important that the pattern's finished surface is smooth to facilitate the removal of the mould when laminated. In addition, it is essential that there are no undercuts.

An undercut is the same as an overhang, where part of the pattern protrudes beyond the surface. If left, it would prevent the laminated mould from being removed from the pattern. Where an overhang or undercut has been incorporated intentionally, because it's part of the required shape, the mould must be made in more than one piece to facilitate its removal.

Another means of assisting removal of the laminated mould from the pattern and, in turn, the finished component from the mould, is to give the vertical surfaces of the pattern a slight draught angle, that is an almost imperceptible taper, so that it is very slightly narrower at the top than at the base. This is particularly important on deep moulds or moulds with large vertical surfaces, and should be considered on rectangular or square moulds with sharp corners. A slight draught angle should also be considered if the mould will have deep slots or troughs.

With deep-sided patterns or moulds, or large vertical areas, the pure mechanical hold of the laminated mould to the pattern can make it difficult to remove, because that mechanical hold is maintained until the mould is completely off the pattern. With a slight draught angle, once the initial hold has been broken, the slight taper of the pattern makes it progressively easier to pull the mould off.

Where a sectional mould is required to allow removal of the component, each section of the mould must be laminated separately. To achieve this, material used for the peripheral weirs is attached across the pattern's surface, at the apex of any overhang or undercut.

Release coating

Whether the mould is one piece or sectional, the next stage is to apply the release coating to the entire pattern, weirs and baseboard. This very important task must be carried out with some care. If it is not done well, there is a danger that you will not be able to remove the mould from the pattern when finished.

Failure of the mould to release from the pattern could mean having to start from the beginning again. Obviously, there are differing degrees of release failure. For example, the mould may stick only to portions of the pattern and, when eventually separated, either the mould or pattern, or both, may be repairable. If the surface of the pattern is damaged, the type of repair will depend on the material used to make it in the first place. If the mould is damaged, it usually means filling the damaged area with a gel coat and, when this has cured, rubbing down to the original profile by hand, then polishing. When a partial release failure occurs, the level of damage usually dictates whether or not it is practical to make a repair.

The most widely used method of releasing GRP moulds from patterns is quite simple, but it must be done thoroughly. The technique is to give the pattern six or seven coats of release wax. Each application should be carefully rubbed into the surface, taking care not to miss any small areas, and allowed to stand to give the wax time to harden, after which it should be polished by hand with a soft cloth. Then, the next coat should be applied, and so on until the required number has been added. The time the wax takes to harden will depend on the type used and the atmospheric conditions where the process is being carried out. It is important to allow the wax to harden; failure to do so has the effect of reducing the number of coats, as one application of wax will remove the previous coat.

When the final coat has hardened and been polished out, to be absolutely certain of release, some laminators will give the pattern a coat of PVA (poly vinyl alcohol). If this is to be used, it must be applied with a very soft brush or a pad of soft cloth. As PVA dries to leave a thin membrane, any runs or brush marks will remain, and since the coat forms the outer surface of the pattern, these will be transferred to the mould surface and, in turn, to the surface of the components from that mould. The thin coating of PVA is quite fragile, so care must be taken to prevent it from becoming damaged prior to, and during, application of the gel coat.

While not essential if the wax treatment is carried out correctly, PVA does offer some assurance of release, especially if the pattern does not have a perfect finish. This can be the case if the pattern is an old part that is being copied and cannot have too much preparation work carried out on it. If a porous material has been used for the weirs, it is a good idea to treat them with PVA, even if you have not used it on the rest of the pattern.

PVA air dries, and the time taken will depend on the atmospheric conditions at the time; some types contain a solvent to speed up the drying process. It is also water soluble, and can be removed from the pattern and mould, after they have been separated, by washing in warm soapy water.

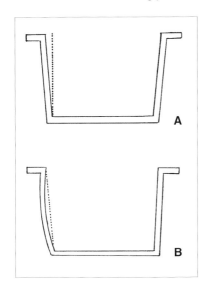

A Incorporating a draught angle (a slight taper) into deep or steep-sided moulds will assist the removal of the finished component. Here, the angle has been exaggerated for the purpose of the diagram; in reality, the angle would be very shallow indeed.

B Here a concavity has formed in what is meant to be a flat-sided mould. This can prevent the removal of the finished component due to the resultant undercut. This type of fault can be caused by a poorly-made pattern or shrinkage of the mould during the cure.

4

Making moulds

When the mould is to be laminated on a pattern, your preparatory work should be checked thoroughly, as both pattern and mould will be at risk if this work has not been carried out properly. Poor preparation could result in a useless mould and the possible loss of the pattern, due to damage if the mould cannot be released from it.

Make sure that there are no undercuts that would prevent the mould from being removed by pure mechanical locking. When the mould is to be made in more than one piece, to facilitate removal from a complex pattern or simply because it is large and removal would be very difficult if it was in one piece, weirs should have been fitted to provide the split lines. Check that these are positioned correctly and, most importantly, that they are attached to the pattern very securely. A difficult situation can arise if any of the weirs come off, or move, once lamination of the mould has begun.

Applying the gel coat

With the pattern fully prepared and treated with release agents, consideration must be given to the first stages of laminating the mould. Stage one is the application of a gel coat to the pattern. It is advisable to tint the gel coat with a purpose-made pigment, and while the choice of colour is not important, it is a good idea to use a colour that will contrast with the colour of the components that ultimately will be made from the mould. For example, if the moulded components are likely to be of a light colour, the mould should be dark. In this way, when gel coating the finished mould to make a component, you will have no trouble in achieving good overall coverage, as any thin or uncoated areas will be obvious.

Pigment is added to the gel coat and mixed in at the same time as the catalyst. Gel coat can be purchased already coloured, but only in large quantities (usually at least 20kg/44lb). Most gel coats, however, are pigmented at the time of application.

The amount of pigment or colouring paste that should be added to the gel coat will depend on the colour itself. This is because some colours are stronger than others. Black, for instance, is very strong and, therefore, will require less pigment than some other colours. Yellow, especially the pale versions, is very weak, so a higher percentage of colouring paste will be needed. That said, aim to use as little colouring paste as possible to achieve the required colour. Too much will have a detrimental effect on the curing of the gel coat, resulting in the finished surface being softer than it should be; in extreme cases, a proper cure may not take place at all.

The recommended maximum amount of pigment is 10% by weight. In most cases, the percentage required will be much less. A good way of achieving the required colour is to add a little of the colouring paste at a time to the gel coat and spread a small amount on something of a contrasting colour. You will then see when the density of the chosen colour has reached the point where it gives a good solid looking colour. When you have obtained the colour you require, add the catalyst. To achieve an acceptable deep colour with some pigments, a second gel coat will be needed. This should be applied when the first coat has almost cured.

When applying a gel coat, its thickness is not critical, but it must be thick enough to prevent the glass fibres from reaching the mould surface. Another advantage of a reasonably thick gel coat is that it allows for polishing the mould surface after removal from the pattern. It also permits the mould to be repolished after considerable use, either as a refurbishment or to remove minor surface damage or wear.

However, it is very important not to apply too thick a gel coat in one go, as this can lead to shrinkage as the gel coat cures, resulting in voids or pockets forming in corners and areas of deep detail within the mould. One common area for this type of error to occur is where there is a sharp edge or ridge as part of any detailing. At this point, the gel coat is likely to be thickest, and as it shrinks, the detail will be lost.

Therefore, to achieve a good thick gel coat, you will need to apply it in two stages, allowing the first to reach a level of cure where the surface is very slightly tacky. At this stage, the second application of gel coat can be made without fear of it disturbing the first.

It is difficult to measure the thickness of wet applications of gel coat. There is a method that relies on a comb-like tool with graduated tooth length, but it is hardly worth the effort. Through using these materials, you will soon be able to judge what makes a suitable application thickness.

An excellent way of learning what the gel coat thickness should look like is to aim to apply it at the rate of 300g/sq.m (1oz/sq.ft). This is not super critical, as the coat is bound to be thinner in some places and thicker in others. To achieve this, measure the approximate area of the pattern or the section of the pattern about to be gel coated and convert the answer to square metres or square feet. Multiply this by 300g or 1oz to obtain the weight to be applied to that area. Add a little extra to allow for the residue that will be left in the mixing pot and on the application brush.

Weigh out the correct amount of gel coat into a suitable mixing vessel, then calculate the amount of catalyst needed and add this to the gel coat. The ratio of catalyst to gel coat will depend on the volume of the intended mix, the size of the area to be coated or the complexity of the pattern's shape. As applying gel coat is a fairly simple and quick process, a complex pattern shape is unlikely to affect the application time and, therefore, this will be a minor consideration. If the area being coated is large and likely to take a long time to cover (as a rough guide, over 30 minutes), the time in which the gel coat begins to go off will be important. Temperature also has an effect on the time the mixed gel coat remains usable, so if the component is large, or the temperature is high, the amount of catalyst to gel coat should be kept at the lower end of the recommended mixing ratio.

With most gel coat resins, the amount of catalyst required will be 1½-2%. Some suppliers specify up to 3%, but this would result in a very quick

The GRP body of this race car was made in sections. These were finished in self-coloured gel coat.

gel time, that is the period during which the mixed gel coat remains usable. With a large mix, say about 2kg (4½lb) or more, the percentage of catalyst should be about 1%. In fact, 1-1½% is a good average ratio for most applications. With experience, you will soon discover the ideal mixing ratio for the job in hand. This ratio can be altered to reduce the time that the gel has to stand before the next coat can be applied, or laminating can be carried out.

A mixing ratio chart will be available from the materials supplier, and if a catalyst measure is used, there will be no problem in determining the correct amount of catalyst to add, as it will be dispensed automatically.

With the catalyst metered into the gel coat, the two should be mixed together. Simply stirring by hand is a satisfactory method of mixing, but it is essential to carry this out thoroughly, as the catalyst must combine with all of the gel coat resin in the mix. The percentage of catalyst is so small that, if not stirred enough, it will not reach all the gel coat mix. If higher percentages of catalyst are being added, or the temperature where the work is being carried out is much above normal room temperature, make sure the mixing process does not take too long, as the pot life begins soon after the catalyst is added. 'Pot life' is the term used to describe the time the mixed gel coat remains usable, that is before it starts to gel, which is the first stage of cure. This is indicated by the mix beginning to thicken and becoming difficult to apply.

Brushing on the gel coat can be done quite quickly; there is no need to brush in one direction, or smooth out brush marks, as you would do when applying normal paint. Simply aim to apply a good overall coating, reasonably evenly dispersed. If you have calculated the approximate amount of gel coat for the area to be coated, the thickness will be correct when this has been evenly distributed over the entire area. It is very important not to allow too great a build-up of gel coat in any tight corners, or the mould detail to become overfilled. As explained earlier, this can lead to shrinkage in these areas, or even cracking of the gel coat upon final cure.

The cockpit and tail section, shown with its mould.

The centre section of the body after removal from the mould.

The nose section of the race car with the split mould from which it was made.

A simple male pattern (white) together with the resultant female mould (black).

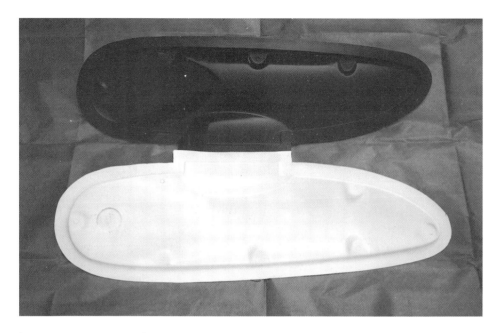

In extreme cases of gel coat build-up, it is possible for the gel coat to be degraded by the excessive heat generated as it cures, giving rise to an exotherm. However, it must be said that this form of degradation is rare with gel coats.

When the gel coat mixture has been brushed evenly over the required area, it should be left at ambient temperature to cure. At this point, any brushes used in the process should have all excess gel coat squeezed out of their bristles and be left in a vessel with some acetone. Other items used should be wiped clean and made ready for the next coat.

As a mould is being made, and it is advisable for moulds to have a reasonably thick gel coat, this can be achieved with a second application of gel coat. When the first is sufficiently cured that it feels very slightly tacky, yet can be touched with a clean finger without any gel coat sticking to that finger, and without the finger leaving a mark, you can apply the second coat. It is important not to attempt this second application too soon, as it will disturb the first, which can lead to a poorly finished gel coat with very thin and very thick areas.

The second coat is applied in exactly the same way as the first. Again, remember to clean your brushes, etc, as soon as possible after finishing. If they will not be used any more that day, remove the gel coat by putting them in acetone, or any other cleaner your supplier might suggest, then wash them out in warm soapy water. It is a good idea to look after your laminating brushes. Not only will this save you money, but also brushes seem to get better after a little use.

Leave the second application of gel coat until it is almost tack-free before going on to the next stage. If circumstances prevent you from doing this until after the gel coat cures fully, or reaches the tack-free stage, provided the delay is of no more than a day or two, in most cases it will be perfectly acceptable to laminate the next stage.

If you are making a one-piece mould, you will have gel coated the entire pattern and out on to the overruns formed by the base board and weirs. If the mould is to be of the split type, with two or more sections, you should have gel coated one section, usually the largest, out on to the base board and up on to the weir that is to form the split line. In the latter case, this first section should be laminated in the same manner as a complete one-piece mould.

Adding surface tissue

The first stage of laminating the mould is to apply a surface tissue. This has three advantages: being very thin, the tissue will form readily to the surface of the pattern, following any fine detail; it prevents air from becoming trapped directly behind the gel coat; and it prevents the pronounced fibres of the chopped strand matt from showing through the gel coat.

The mixing ratio of polyester resin for the laminating process is the same as for the gel coat, that is 1-2% of catalyst to resin. Again, the volume of the mix and the temperature where the work is being carried out will affect the pot life of the mixed resin, as will the types of resin and catalyst being used. In most cases, 1-1½% of catalyst will be suitable. As with the gel coat, mixing must be thorough, as a very small amount of catalyst must be distributed completely throughout a much larger volume of resin.

The amount of resin you mix will depend on the amount of glass matt you intend laminating at each stage. To arrive at the amount of resin required, you must measure approximately the area of glass matt to be laminated. The weight of glass matt purchased will be known, and the ratio of resin to glass for most laminating is 2.5 to 1. As an example, if you are to laminate a square metre of glass matt, and the matt is of the 300g/sq.m type, the amount of resin required is 750g. It must be added, at this point, that when a laminate is to be very thick (6mm/¼in or more), where you will be putting up to three plies into the lamination at a time, the resin-to-glass ratio can be brought down to 2 to 1.

The sample calculation given is for one ply only; when a lamination is beginning to progress, you will be putting on more than one ply at a time.

However, at the first stage of mould lamination, when only a layer of surface tissue is being applied, there is no point in trying to work out the amount of resin required, as the tissue is so light and requires so little resin to wet it out. In this case, simply mix sufficient resin to be able to

This mould has been designed to produce a one-piece car body—minus doors, of course.

paint a generous coat over the area to be laminated. With a little experience, you will soon be able to make a reasonable guess at the amount of resin to mix for most laminating tasks. Calculating the amount is good experience for the beginner, and is useful to anyone when there are repetitive laminates to be made, as it can help eliminate waste.

With the resin mixed, you can begin the lamination. To do this, brush a generous wet coat over the area to be laminated. Then drape or lay the surface tissue over the resin. The tissue can be cut or torn into suitably sized or shaped pieces to make it easier to position. When the tissue is put on in sections like this, there is no need to worry about achieving even overlaps, or the number of overlaps. The tissue is so thin that there will be no significant build-up of thickness where it does overlap.

When the tissue is in place, use a paint brush with a stippling, or dabbing, action to push it on to the pattern's surface. This stippling action will bring the resin through the tissue, allowing it to lay on the gel coated surface. It is essential to ensure that the tissue is in complete contact with the surface being covered, and that no air has been trapped under the tissue, as this could lead to blisters forming in the surface of the finished mould. Close attention must be paid to any tight corners or sharp detail; the same stippling action will ensure that the tissue is forced into every crevice. This will be comparatively easy, as the tissue is so thin. It will be obvious when the tissue is completely wetted out with resin: the colour will change from the normal milky white to the colour of the mixed resin, that is almost transparent. At this stage, it will be easy to see if any air bubbles are trapped under the tissue. Further stippling with the brush will force the trapped air through the tissue. You must take the time to do this if you want a good mould.

Dealing with tight corners

Tight corners and sharp detail must also be considered at this point with regard to laminating the next stage, using chopped strand matt. The tissue will have followed all the contours of the pattern without any problems, but the chopped strand matt may be reluctant to stay in these very tight corners while the resin is curing, due to the natural stiffness of the glass fibres. To overcome this problem, it is advisable to pre-fill any tight corners at the tissue stage. There are two widely used methods for doing this: one is to use lengths of glass roving, the other is to laminate narrow strips of chopped strand matt.

When using glass roving, the lengths should be wetted out with resin before laminating them in place. To do this, you can lay them out on a sheet of polythene and paint them with the resin, or a neat method is to dip a brush in the resin and simply pull the roving through the brush. Take the lengths of wetted roving and place them in the tight corners on top of the wetted tissue layer. Dab the roving into place, using the brush. This will have the effect of filling in the tight corners and crevices, producing a larger radius to which the heavier chopped strand matt can be formed.

The other method of pre-filling corners has the same effect of increasing their radius, but instead or roving, strips of chopped strand matt of various widths are used. Start with a width of approximately l0mm (⅜in) and position it, in its dry state, on top of the wet tissue on one surface leading into the corner, with its edge placed into the corner. Then wet out with

A complex multi-piece mould. The top section (with single hole) splits in half; the lower section splits in half and through the centre of each of the four holes.

When using this multi-piece mould, the two main sections are gel coated and laminated in their separate halves, then bolted together. A subsequent lamination is applied through the holes to join the sections of the component together.

The component produced by the multi-piece mould. Note the 'flash' lines where the sections of mould meet. These will be trimmed off.

The mould for a domestic
shower liner.

resin, using the same stippling action as before. Place the next strip, of the
same width, with its edge tight into the corner on the other surface. Don't
allow the strips to run from one surface on to the other, as they will not stay
there, causing a void. Take another strip that is narrower than the first and
place in the corner as before. Wet out, then repeat on the other surface.
If the chopped strand matt is of 450g/sq.m (1½oz/sq.ft) or less, repeat the
process for a third time, making sure that these final strips are narrower
than the previous pair. You will find that with each strip of glass matt
applied, the resin takes a short while to wet it out. The type of binder in the
glass matt will affect this time, but it is always quite quick and should not
hold up laminating. As with glass tissue, the matt will be fully wetted out
when its milky white appearance disappears and it takes on the colour of
the resin.

When dabbing the last strip into place, you will find that the fully wetted out glass matt blends into a nicely radiused corner without the fibres
having to run around the original sharp angle, while the stepped effect
caused by the differing widths of strip results in a tapering of the surfaces
on each side of the corner. This prevents the formation of a pronounced
step to laminate over later and, in turn, any possibility of a ridge forming
in the finished laminate.

These techniques of dealing with tight corners and sharp detail are
easy to carry out and well worth the effort. Both methods are given as
basic guides. The width of strips, for example, is unimportant; in fact, even
if the strips vary in width, it doesn't matter. The important requirement is
to fill any tight corner with wetted out glass without the fibres having to
form around the corner. With a little experience, you will get to know the
type of corner and sharp detail that normal glass fibre matt will follow when
wet, without requiring this additional attention.

When the tissue layer has been completed, and any tight corners or
sharp detail filled, the lamination should be left to cure partially before
going on to the next stage. This can be carried out when the resin has

reached a point where just a slight tack can be felt, but nothing sticks to your finger when you pull it away.

Building up the lamination

The next task is to apply the first ply of chopped strand matt. Whatever the shape of the pattern, it is advisable to use a light matt for this, as it will form more readily to the contours, in a similar fashion to the tissue. This is particularly important if the pattern is a complex shape. Ideally, make this first ply from material of 300g/sq.m (1oz/sq.ft), but certainly not more than 450g/sq.m (1½oz/sq.ft). Both are commonly available weights.

Before mixing the laminating resin, cut the glass matt to size and shape. Experienced laminators often tear the matt into suitably sized pieces: tearing gives a very ragged edge to the matt, which helps to prevent distinct ridges from forming in the laminate. The position of each overlap is not critical, and as there will be several layers of the glass matt, they can be in slightly different positions for each layer, so no very large ridges will be produced. Therefore, you may find it easier to cut the glass with a craft knife.

The number of pieces of glass matt used to cover a pattern is unimportant, so choose a size that is easy to handle. To some extent, the shape of the pattern will dictate the way in which the glass matt is cut. If the pattern is large and of a simple shape, the glass can be cut into large, suitably shaped pieces. When the pattern has a complex shape, or features sharp detail, the matt needs to be in smaller pieces and shapes that allow it to be laminated around the shape without the need for a lot of folds. Folds should be avoided, as they are not easy to flatten during the laminating process and can result in voids in the finished laminate. Once you begin laminating, it will soon become obvious what can be done with the glass matt during lamination and what can't. This will give you an idea of how to cut the matt to suit the job in hand.

The moulded shower liner.

Mix enough resin to wet out the glass prepared for the first layer of chopped strand matt, adding 1-2% of catalyst, as described previously. Brush a thick coat over the pattern, or the area of the pattern to be laminated. If, by this time, the tissue layer (or any other layer in the laminate) has become completely dry to the touch, you can still proceed with the lamination provided a very generous coating of resin is brushed on before the next layer of glass is added.

Lay the pre-cut glass matt, or one or more pieces if in sections, on the wet resin. Then use a laminating roller to roll the matt into the resin. There is no particular pattern or direction in which the glass must be rolled, but you should ensure that all of it is forced into the resin; apply firm, but not heavy, pressure to the roller. Where areas of the pattern's shape prevent the roller from being used, such as in tight corners, narrow channels, etc, employ a paint brush and the previously described stippling action to force the matt into the resin. The rolling and stippling will bring the resin up through the glass matt, wetting it out. It would be ideal if there was sufficient resin in the brushed-on coat to wet out the glass matt fully, but this is seldom the case, and more resin is likely to need adding. This should be done with the brush, applying it to the matt with the stippling action, as before. When the matt appears to be wet, leave it for a short while—one or two minutes is enough. Then, using the roller and brush, consolidate the layer fully. Again, the disappearance of the matt's milky white colour will indicate that it is fully wetted out.

Any pockets of trapped air may be visible at this stage and, if seen, they must be removed by dabbing with the brush to bring the air up through the matt. Pay particular attention to tight corners and sharp detail, where the glass matt will form least readily, making sure that it is completely in contact with the tissue layer underneath. If the matt is being put on in sections, pay a little extra attention to the overlaps to ensure complete consolidation and that there is no trapped air.

When the lamination of this layer is complete, leave it until almost tack-free before applying the next. In the meantime, wash your brushes in a suitable solvent.

At some point, the thickness of the intended mould must be decided upon, as this will be controlled by the number of plies in the lamination. The number of plies required for a given thickness is determined by the thickness, or weight, of the chopped strand matt.

There are no set rules governing the thickness of a mould, and experienced laminators will have their own ideas on the subject. Various considerations must be taken into account, however. If very tight dimensional accuracy is called for, the mould should be thick and, therefore, rigid. If the finished component will be light in weight and would not withstand much leverage to remove it from the mould, a mould that can be twisted or distorted slightly will aid its removal. With a large mould, the wall thickness must be increased to maintain the intended shape and dimensions. Other points to consider are that moulds with simple shapes will be more flexible, while those with complex shapes will automatically stiffen due to the shape itself.

All this would appear to make the decision on mould wall thickness difficult to reach, but in fact, the thickness is not that critical. As a guide, aim to make the mould wall thickness approximately three times the thickness of the component that will be made in it. To arrive at the amount of chopped strand matt needed to achieve the intended thickness, assume that 400g/sq.m (1¼oz/sq.ft) of chopped strand matt results in a laminated thickness of 1mm (¹⁄₂₅in). There is no point in measuring the thickness of the dry matt and working from there, as wet hand laminating moves the chopped strands about. Moreover, the difference in individual laminating techniques will cause the finished thickness to vary, and most finished laminates will display some degree of thickness variation.

Assuming 400g equals a 1mm thickness over a square metre (or 1¼oz, ¹⁄₂₅in over a square foot) is a good general guide, but don't worry if the matt you have does not calculate to exactly the desired thickness you want. Simply aim for the nearest possible amount. It may help if you have more than one weight of glass matt at your disposal, which may be the case if you are using a lightweight matt as the first ply after the tissue.

When the first layer of glass matt is almost tack-free, you may proceed with the second ply. If the pattern is of a complex shape, or has sharp detail, it is advisable to use lightweight glass matt for this second ply, too. If, however, the pattern is of a relatively simple shape, the second ply can be of a heavier matt, but at this early stage, it is not a good idea to use glass matt with a weight of more than 450g/sq.m (1½oz/sq.ft).

The second ply is laminated in exactly the same manner as the first.

The mould for a section of a children's slide. Polyester is a good choice for outdoor GRP applications, as it weathers well.

Since it will be applied to the rough surface of part-cured chopped strand matt, make sure that no air is trapped beneath the matt you are laminating. Employ the roller to consolidate the laminate, but as it may ride over the high spots of the previous ply, go back over the surface with a paint brush, using the normal stippling action. This works very well as a consolidating method. In fact, in areas where the roller can't be used, the brush is the only means of consolidation. In theory, it is possible to laminate with only a brush, and in professional GRP workshops, many small intricate laminates are consolidated completely by this method. Don't dismiss the roller, however, as it is an important tool that should be utilized to the full on most laminates.

Again, when the second ply is almost tack-free, the third ply can be laminated. At this point, the intended thickness of the laminate must be considered. Now that the tissue and first two plies are in place, further plies may be added at the rate of more than one at a time. Some experienced laminators will often put on three plies in one go, but others never put down more than two at a time. When putting down multi-plies, it is important to remember not to use the higher percentage of catalyst, as there is a danger of the resin beginning to go off before the lamination is complete, which could be a disaster if some of the laminate was still unconsolidated.

If the first two plies utilized 300g/sq.m (1oz/sq.ft) chopped strand matt, the approximate thickness of the mould wall will be 1.5mm (¹⁄₁₆in) at this stage. Two more plies of the same material will result in a wall thickness of approximately 3mm (⅛in). For many moulds, this would be thick enough, but the mould would still be slightly flexible, which can be an asset when it comes to removing a component made in the mould. As mentioned before, the shape and size of the mould will have a decided effect on its stiffness. In most cases, moulds are not intended to be flexible, so it may be necessary to add another ply, or even two. If heavier glass matt is at hand, however, the number of extra plies can be reduced. With many large moulds, the wall thickness should be 5-6mm (⅕-¼in), while an extra large mould (for a big boat, perhaps) may need a wall thickness of 10 or 12mm (⅖ or ½in). When much thicker moulds of this type are required, it is advisable to use heavier matt after the first two layers to reduce the total number of plies required: 600g/sq.m (2oz/sq.ft) is widely used and, in some cases, 900g/sq.m (3oz/sq.ft).

If you intend laminating the third and fourth plies in one go, apply the former exactly as before, making sure that it is consolidated fully and formed into all the corners and detail of the pattern. Then continue to laminate the fourth ply while the third is still wet. In most cases, there should be enough resin for both plies.

Allow these two plies to become almost tack-free before repeating the process, or allow them to cure fully if you have achieved the required wall thickness and the mould is of the one-piece type. The finished mould should be left at ambient temperature for five or six days before attempting to remove it from the pattern, unless there are facilities available that allow a post cure, that is holding the mould and pattern at a steady specified temperature.

Below **This gel coated mould is for an electronics cover.**

Below right **The electronics cover after removal from the mould, but before being trimmed.**

Post cure

Polyester resin systems are very slow to reach the fully cured state, which provides a large percentage of their potential strength. This can take weeks, or even months, and the post cure shortens this period. It also offers a means of determining when the cure is complete; there is no way of telling when an ambient-temperature cure is complete. However, almost all polyester cures take place at ambient temperature, which is perfectly

STIFFENING RIBS

A Paper rope can be used to form laminated stiffening ribs on the back of a large mould, one or two plies of chopped strand matt being laminated over the rope. Paper rope is available in different diameters: the larger the mould, the larger the diameter of rope. With very large stiffeners, a slightly thicker laminate is used. It is important to allow the laminated mould to cure before adding the stiffening ribs. This will prevent contraction of the curing rib from distorting the mould.
B Stiffening ribs can also be formed with foam cores.

acceptable, provided sufficient time is allowed. With a large mould, you may have no option.

If a post cure is possible, the newly laminated mould should be left at ambient temperature for at least 48 hours, followed by five hours at 45-60°C (113-140°F). Before embarking on a post cure, you should consider whether the pattern will withstand the temperature and, if the pattern is required again, whether the heat will cause any distortion. If an oven is available for post curing, but the pattern won't withstand the temperature, the mould can be post cured after removal from the pattern, but this should be after spending five or six days at ambient temperature.

Adding stiffening ribs

If the mould is quite large, or if it has large flat areas, to avoid the need for very thick walls to stabilize these areas, it is common practice to add additional stiffness to the mould after it has been laminated. There are various ways of doing this. One employs paper rope, which is made for the purpose. Lengths of the rope are laid across the back of the mould and chopped strand matt is laminated over them to form ribs. Two plies of moderate-weight matt will be sufficient. On a very large mould, lengths of paper rope should be laminated across the width and length. Other materials can also be used to form stiffening ribs, such as rigid foam, cardboard tubing, wood and metal tubing, although the last is not recommended, as its expansion rate differs from the GRP and can cause a mould to distort. In fact, the material used to form stiffening ribs can be almost anything, as it is the tube-like shape formed by the laminated glass matt that adds the stiffness. It is important not to add any stiffening ribs until the mould is part cured (for at least 24 hours), otherwise some distortion may occur.

Multi-section moulds

So far, we have considered the lamination of a one-piece mould only. If, however, you are making a multi-section mould, the task is more complex. In this case, the first section will have been laminated exactly as described for a one-piece mould, but only as far as, and on to, the first weir, which forms the joint of the split mould.

The next step is to sand the rough edges of the lamination back to the weir, then remove the weir, washing off the PVA with warm soapy water. At this point, it must be decided whether some form of locating device will be needed to hold the sections of the mould in proper alignment. The need for location points is very important on large moulds, where the slightest bend or minor distortion would result in a very poor joint line on the component being made. However, it is excellent practice to provide some form of positive location on all moulds, especially if they are intended for repeat use, and there are various methods of doing this.

LOCATING DEVICES

A A peg-and-ring location for the sections of a split mould. The pegs are laminated in at various intervals around the mould's edge or the weirs. The rings are placed on the pegs and the next part of the mould laminated around them. Sometimes, this type of locating device is bonded into the finished mould by drilling their locations prior to separating the mould halves. The pegs and rings are usually made of steel.

B Ferrule-type inserts can be bonded into the cured mould. The mould flange is drilled to the size of the barrel and the ferrule bonded in using two-part epoxy adhesive. The barrel length is adjusted to suit the thickness of the mould flange prior to bonding in. The result is a metal lined hole that will resist wear and give accurate location of mould sections when used in conjunction with close fitting bolts. Ferrule-type inserts can be aluminium or steel; it is not advisable to use brass, as this does not bond very well.

C A conical, locating former stuck to the pattern flange or weir prior to laminating the first half of the mould. These formers can be bought or made. Wax and plastic are the most widely used materials, as both are self-releasing.

D A section through a finished mould, where the former has resulted in a recess in the mould flange, which is laminated into when laying up the second half. The mould sections are clamped together during component manufacture by nuts and bolts.

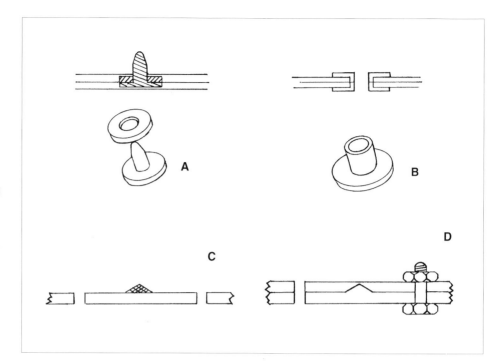

In some cases, when multi-section moulds are being made, the joining flanges are drilled for bolts before the sections are removed from the pattern. This simple method works quite well, provided the bolts are a close fit in the holes. But a great improvement on this method is to use metal bolt-hole liners. These are available from most GRP suppliers and consist of a metal sleeve with a shoulder at one end. While the mould is on the pattern, the joining flanges are drilled to the sleeve size. Then, using two-part epoxy adhesive applied to the sleeve and shoulder, the liners are bonded in to each half of the flange. Finally, bolts that match the size of the sleeve holes are fitted and tightened just enough to hold the liners in place while the epoxy sets. The use of these metal inserts prevents the GRP flange holes from wearing and maintains a more accurate location of the mould joint.

Another form of location for sectional moulds is to incorporate protrusions and matching recesses on the faces of the mating flanges. There are several methods of achieving this. One simple, often used technique is to drill recesses into the face of the mould flange prior to laminating the next section. The lamination then forms into the recesses, resulting in a plug-and-socket type of location. The recesses can be made with a drill countersink or a conical drill burr. They must be deep enough to provide positive location of the sections, but must be free from undercuts.

Another way of forming this type of location is to stick recess forming plugs on to the weir, then laminate over them. The plugs are removed along with the weir, resulting in moulded recesses in the face of the flange. When the next section is laminated, the locating plugs are formed. The advantage of this method is that it is easier to achieve a nice conical shape to each recess without the need for drilling. Although material suppliers can provide plastic forms for this purpose, it is a simple task to make them from plastic, hard wax or metal. It is always better to use a non-porous material, however, as sealing a number of such small plugs is tedious and unreliable.

Metal plug-and-socket locators are also available. Normally made from steel or aluminium, these consist of a tube-like socket and a matching plug or peg, both with a shoulder at one end. Prior to laminating the first section of the mould, the shoulders of the sockets are stuck to the weirs. These are laminated over and become an integral part of the mould. When the first section of the mould has been completed and the weirs have been removed, the plug portions of the locators are placed in the sockets, which now form an integral part of the joining flange. The plugs will be laminated into the flange of the next section. The result is a very positive and permanent method of mould section location.

It must be remembered that where locating devices are stuck on to, or drilled into, the weirs, this must be done prior to the mould release agent being applied, so that they receive the same release treatment as the pattern and weirs. However, metal plug-and-socket locators must not have any release materials applied to them, as they will be laminated into the mould flanges.

When considering the use of mould section locating devices, and deciding on a suitable type, several points will affect your decision. For example, large moulds only need a very small amount of distortion to produce a very poor joint line, and this distortion could be the result of a tiny amount of shrinkage over a large area. If close tolerances are imposed on the moulded component, it is important to ensure positive location for the mould sections. Another good reason for providing positive location is a thin mould wall. The choice of a thin mould wall may have been made for economic reasons (to save on materials, or because the mould is only intended to have a short life), but in most cases, the purpose of a thinner mould wall is to provide a more flexible mould as an aid to removing the finished component. This method is often employed when the intended component is to be a lightweight structure and will not be strong enough to be removed from the mould by the normal methods. If a multi-section mould is flexible, good location becomes very important.

Having taken a decision on mould section location, you can laminate the remainder of the sections in turn, using exactly the same method as the first. Remember to remove the weirs when they have been laminated on one side, and make sure that the mould flange exposed by the removal

A pattern, mould and finished component. The pattern is on the right, the split mould on the left and the moulded fan duct at the front.

of the weir is given the correct release treatment prior to laminating the next section.

When all the sections have been laminated, and any additional stiffening has been added, the mould should be left for at least two or three days if a post cure is planned. This must take place at 40-60°C (113-140°F) for five or six hours. If post curing facilities are not available, the mould should be left for at least six days to allow it to reach a full ambient-temperature cure prior to proceeding with the next stage, which is the removal of the mould from the pattern.

Removing the mould from the pattern

When the new mould is ready for removal from the pattern, trim the edge and any joining flanges first. An electric sander with a fairly coarse disc is ideal for this. Sand back to leave a clean edge and, on multi-section moulds, sufficient flange width to accommodate the holes for the bolts that will clamp the sections together. These can be drilled next. The size of the bolts is not critical; as a guide use 6mm (¼in) bolts for small moulds, and 12mm (½in) bolts for large moulds.

There are no set rules governing the number of bolts to fit or their spacing, but on long flanges, spacing the holes approximately 100mm (4in) apart works well. However, if you have made a thin flexible mould, it is a good idea to place the clamp bolts closer together. A complex shape with several sections and their related flanges will induce extra stiffness, so fewer bolts will be needed.

With flanges trimmed and bolt holes drilled, the mould can be removed from the pattern. The most widely used method of doing this is to drive tapered wedges between the flanges. The wedges are best made of wood or plastic, and should have a shallow taper.

When using wedges to separate mould sections, they should be tapped in gently to a depth of approximately 12mm (½in). At the base flange of a multi-section mould, it is a good idea to begin inserting the wedges close to the flanges that form the mould joins, as the mould will be stiffer at these points. The number of wedges used is unimportant, but tap them in approximately 200-250mm (8-10in) apart. If several wedges have been tapped partially in, but the mould has not started to come off the pattern, give the mould, or section, a series of sharp blows with a rubber mallet, spreading them over the entire area of the mould or section. The shock imposed by the mallet blows may be sufficient to cause the mould to separate from the pattern. If separation still has not occurred, gently tap the wedges further in and, if necessary, use the mallet again. This should separate the mould and allow it to be taken off the pattern.

If the mould is particularly reluctant to separate from the pattern, and the latter has been given a coat of PVA release agent, provided the mould is not too large, pouring warm soapy water through the openings made by the wedges will dissolve some of the PVA. This will assist the separation process.

On large moulds, or moulds with reasonably large flat or shallow curved areas, another aid can be used to assist separation: compressed air. To utilize this method, it is necessary to fit connectors into the mould near the centre of each large area. These connectors are usually purpose-made items available from most GRP suppliers, or they can be easily

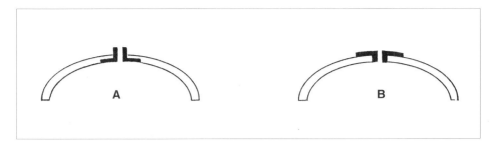

fabricated. All that is required is a metal device to which an air line can be connected, with an integral flange so that it can be laminated in when the mould is being made, or bonded in after the mould has been laminated. Drilling for these connectors after the mould has been laminated usually means that the holes will enter the pattern slightly, and if the pattern is required again, obviously they will have to be repaired.

Air connectors put in to release a mould from the pattern can also be used to assist in the removal of components made in the mould. In some cases, air assistance may not be used to remove the mould from the pattern, but connectors will be put in the completed mould to help release components. Remember that a component made in a mould is usually of much lighter construction than the mould itself, so less force will be required to remove it. However, most GRP mould and component construction can be carried out without the need for air assisted release, so don't be deterred if this facility is not available.

Once the wedges have begun to separate the mould and pattern, the remainder of the task should be quite easy. With the mould, or section of mould, off the pattern, it can be prepared for use.

Preparing the mould for use

Wash the mould or section with warm soapy water to remove the PVA release coating. Then dry it thoroughly before applying a solid wax release agent, which is the most reliable method to use if applied correctly. As stated in Chapter 2, the wax should be silicone-free and applied to the manufacturer's instructions.

If the mould is sectional, the joining flanges must be waxed prior to bolting the sections together. Some people only apply two or three coats of wax to the flange faces, but six or seven will be better, as this is the recommended minimum number of wax applications for the mould itself to prepare it for laminating the first component.

With a multi-section mould, this application of wax can only be carried out on the main area of the mould after the sections have been bolted together, which can be done when the flange faces have been waxed. In this situation, prior to any further waxing, it is common practice to seal the joints between the sections, on the mould face side, with modelling clay. This will make the mould join lines less obvious on the finished component. Modelling clay can also be used to form temporary plugs in any air release holes if these have been incorporated.

The new mould is waxed in exactly the same way as the pattern was, that is the wax is carefully applied over the entire assembled mould, including any modelling clay used to seal the joints between the sections of a sectional mould. Don't try to cover too large an area in one go. Using a soft pad of cloth, rub the wax thoroughly into an area that is comfortable

Compressed-air connectors can be used to assist removal of large components from moulds. A Ferrule connectors can be laminated into the mould during construction. This type of connector is usually steel or aluminium. It is stuck to the pattern, or held in place on a peg, then laminated in. These connectors can have male or femal threads to take whatever type of compressed-air fittings are available.

B This type of compressed-air connecting ferrule is bonded into the mould after it has been made. A hole is drilled to the barrel size and the ferrule bonded in using two-part epoxy adhesive. If steel is used, it is a good idea to shot blast the ferrules or, if this is not possible, abrade and degrease them. If aluminium is used, it should be etched before bonding. An etching fluid used before painting alloys is ideal. Light abrasion and degreasing is better than doing nothing.

This sequence of photos shows the stages in the manufacture of a typical GRP mould. Here, the pattern has been completed and is awaiting application of the release agent.

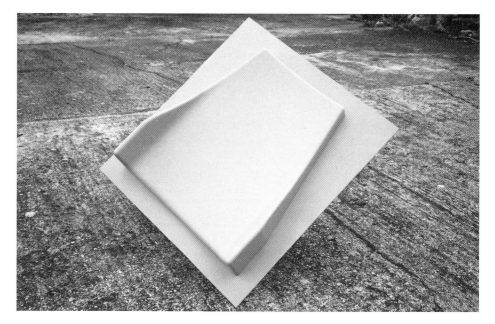

The pattern is waxed and given a coat of PVA release agent.

The first stage in making the mould is to apply a gel coat to the pattern.

After applying a layer of glass tissue, the first ply of chopped strand matt can be added. Here, it is being wetted out with resin. To make the resin visible for the photograph, a pigment has been mixed into it.

The back of the completed mould prior to trimming.

The face of the mould after removal from the pattern. Once the mould has been trimmed, it should be washed with water to remove all traces of the PVA release agent.

ADDITIONS TO MOULDS

A A typical mould section with a flat plate added to form a return flange on the moulded component. This plate can be bolted or clamped in place and can be made from thick GRP laminate or metal (usually aluminium).

B The mould with a laminated component in place. The return flanges can be wet-trimmed back to the plate so that minimal finishing will be required upon removal from the mould.

C In this case, a plate has been added to form a moulded edge to the component. Again, it can be bolted or clamped in place.

D The mould with laminated component in place.

E The finished component with moulded edges.

F A return flange allows two halves of a hollow component to be joined by adhesive.

G Alternatively, a return flange allows a component to be attached to a surface by adhesive or bolts.

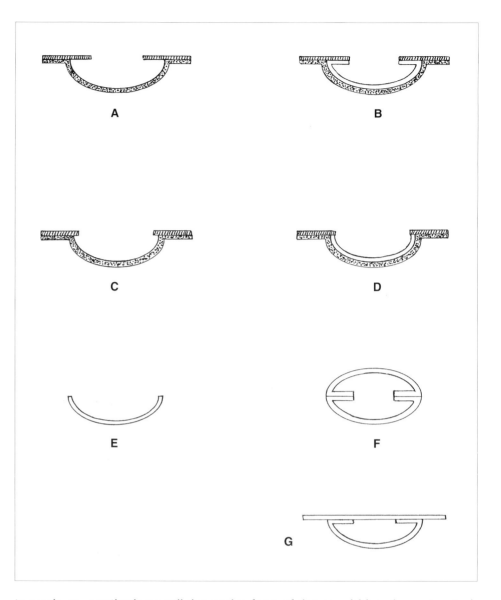

to work on, continuing until the entire face of the mould has been treated. Then leave the wax to harden. The time required will depend on the type and make of wax, and the atmospheric conditions at the time. It can vary considerably, but approximately two hours should be sufficient. When hard, the waxed surface should be polished with a soft dry cloth, then repeat the process for the next coat. With a new mould, apply seven coats of wax before any laminating takes place. Try to prevent the build up of wax, which can easily occur in corners and recesses of the mould.

Seven applications of wax should be sufficient to prepare the mould for the application of the gel coat, but with new moulds, some experienced laminators will also apply a coat of PVA before moulding the first component. This does ensure complete and easy release, but a disadvantage is that it is difficult to apply a thin smooth overall coat, since the PVA tends to run easily and migrate from some areas. Any runs, brush marks or areas where the PVA has puddled will dry to become surface irregularities in the mould, and will be transferred to the surface finish of the component. Such blemishes would be shallow and, if the finished component was painted, they would not be a problem. However, if the proposed component was to be self-coloured, the blemishes could spoil the appearance. They could be polished out with cutting compound and a polishing mop, but that would mean polishing the entire component to maintain a uniform surface appearance.

As there are no hard and fast rules governing the use of this PVA coat, the user must weigh the pros and cons before deciding. It certainly will be worthwhile when the intended component is of complex shape, or has sharp and deep detail. If PVA is to be used, the best results are often achieved by applying it with a pad of soft lint-free material. Alternatively, the PVA may be sprayed on, but preventing runs can be difficult.

At this stage, whether the mould is one piece or sectional, it is ready for laminating the first component.

Repairing defects

Your newly completed mould will always reflect the effort put into its manufacture. A good mould will produce good components, and vice versa, so extra effort at the mould stage will be time well spent. However, regardless of the work put into the construction of a mould, there is always a chance of defects showing up: for example, voids caused by trapped air in very tight corners or extra sharp detail; or sometimes small pieces of mould may be broken off during removal from the pattern. It is important to correct these faults before any waxing takes place.

Where there are voids or missing pieces, the mould must be returned to its original shape, and there are many materials that can be used for this purpose. You can fill the areas with the same gel coat mix as used to surface the mould. This should be allowed to cure fully, after which it can be sanded to the correct profile, then polished. This method does ensure that the repaired surface is identical to the remainder of the mould. The one slight drawback is that, generally, gel coats don't have fantastic adhesive qualities, and unless some effort is put into obtaining a mechanical hold as well, there is a possibility that the repair will be pulled out again.

Another method of repairing defects is to use car body filler. This material has good adhesive qualities and sets very quickly, which can be a bonus if you are in a hurry. However, it tends to be porous, so very close attention should be paid when applying the release to an area repaired in this way. In addition to the several coats of release wax needed prior to using the mould, these repaired areas should be waxed at least once every time a component is taken from the mould.

An excellent method of correcting faults is to use an epoxy-based filler, which is available from most GRP suppliers. The advantage of using epoxy fillers is that they tend to have very good adhesive properties and they produce long lasting repairs. They are also fairly dense, which means that they can be sanded and polished to give quite a good surface finish. The only drawbacks are that the cure time is usually several hours, and they are normally quite expensive in comparison to polyester systems.

A great deal of common sense goes into the manufacture and preparation of a mould. This chapter will serve as a guide to the tasks, but the job in hand will be controlled by the available materials and other factors, such as whether the mould is needed to make only one, or maybe two, components or to make a large number. Other relevant considerations are the equipment available, the level of expertise, and whether the mould is to make components for personal or commercial use.

5

Polyester & vinylester laminating by hand

After applying a release agent to the mould, the component can be laminated in similar fashion to the mould itself. Although six or seven coats of wax should be applied the first time the mould is used, two coats will be sufficient for the second component, and one coat for each component thereafter. When six or seven parts have been made, the wax may be applied for every other moulding. Liquid release agents, however, should always be applied in accordance with the manufacturer's recommendations.

Before actually laminating the component, some important decisions must be made regarding its requirements. Does it need to be strong? Is weight important? Does a special resin have to be used, such as a fire-retardant type or one with particular environmental qualities that has enhanced water resistance? Other points to consider relate to the fibre type. Will chopped strand matt be satisfactory, or does the application make the use of woven fabric a consideration? Another point to take into account is whether the component will be painted after it has been removed from the mould, or be self-coloured, the gel coat being pigmented to the required shade.

Choosing the appropriate materials and methods is not as difficult as the foregoing may make it appear, most GRP applications being straightforward, with readily available materials being perfectly suitable. But it is important to be aware of the specialized materials for the occasion when their use is imperative to the success of the finished component.

The first decision to be made concerns the gel coat colour: if the component is to be self-coloured, it should be pigmented as described in Chapter 2. If the component is to be painted, it is still a good idea to add a pigment. Clear gel coat on laminated glass doesn't look very nice, and the use of a pale grey or white pigment produces a colour that will aid subsequent painting.

The ultimate use of the intended component will have a significant bearing on the thickness of the laminate, although there are no set rules governing this matter. However, apart from affecting the weight, the thickness of a GRP component is not critical, provided it is not too thin. The shape of the component must be considered when deciding on the wall thickness. Components of complex shape, or with deep troughs or channels, will have more inherent stiffness than flat components or those with simple shapes, so their wall thickness can be thinner. If the component is weight sensitive, but still needs to be stiff, the use of woven fabric may be desirable to reduce the wall thickness. If weight is not an important factor, a slightly thicker wall, resulting from the use of chopped strand matt, will be satisfactory.

As a guide to wall thickness, a car body panel, or complete body, would require a thickness of 3mm (⅛in), with slightly thicker areas at mounting points, or where inserts or fittings are to be incorporated in the main lamination. A motor cycle fairing, being smaller and with less surface area, would be satisfactory with a wall thickness of 2mm (¹⁄₁₂in) or so, but the much greater load requirement of a boat, for instance, would require a thicker wall. With boats, the overall size also comes into the equation: a canoe or small rowing boat would need a wall thickness of approximately 4mm (⅛in), while a small motor boat hull would be in the region of 5mm (⅕in) thick. The wall thickness must be increased to match the increase in hull size, reaching 25mm (1in) or more in the case of hulls measuring 30.5m (100ft) long. It must be noted that some of the stiffness and strength in a large boat hull will be provided by internal bulkheads, ribs or frames and, in some cases, built-in buoyancy boxes. When large boat hulls are considered, it is worth seeking the advice of someone involved in the design of boats, to obtain some expert advice on how thick to make the hull, as size is not the only governing factor; the type and conditions of use can also affect the decision.

It is difficult to recommend a wall thickness for other components, as opinions will vary, even among those with experience of GRP, but for most general applications, a wall thickness of between 2 and 4mm (¹⁄₁₂ and ⅛in) will suffice. One important point to consider is that it is not necessary for any component to have a consistent wall thickness. Common practice is to make the wall thicker in strategic areas, that is where there may be a greater load or where fittings are mounted, and at edge flanges.

On large laminated components (truck, bus and train panels for example), the larger unsupported areas of the panels are given extra stiffness by using the thick absorbent core matt described in Chapter 2. One or two plies of this material will be laminated into these areas prior to completing the lamination of the component. This method will help to achieve the required stiffness without the need for a large number of chopped strand matt plies. However, this type of material should not be used to form the main body of the laminate, as its strength would be greatly reduced: core matt must be laminated over to provide extra stiffness. When used in this way, to form the core of a sandwich structure, it keeps the two laminations apart and, being resinated with the laminations on both sides, stabilizes them and helps prevent them from buckling when the component comes under flexing loads.

It is important not to confuse stiffness with strength: it is possible to have a component that is stiff and light, but not necessarily strong. Stiffness is a resistance to bending, and a stiff component can be made with two thin laminations held apart by a central core to form a sandwich structure. However, the two thin laminations forming the skins of the structure would not have much resistance to rough handling. Also, the sandwich structure would normally fail at a much lower bending force than the solid laminate—another feature of strength. Therefore, when considering a component and the way in which it should be made, remember that although the solid laminate may be more flexible, it may also be much

Here, the mould made in Chapter 4 is being gel coated in preparation for laminating the first component. Note the alloy frame bolted to the mould. This will form a moulded edge to the component.

The gel coated mould with pre-cut sections of chopped strand matt ready to be laminated.

The first ply of chopped strand matt being wetted out. The resin has been pigmented to match the colour of the gel coat.

The complete laminated component awaiting cure.

The cured lamination prior to removal from the mould. Note the moulded edge formed by the removable alloy plate.

The reverse of the component after removal from the mould. Note the moulded edge and minimal amount of finishing that will be needed.

The face of the finished GRP
component.

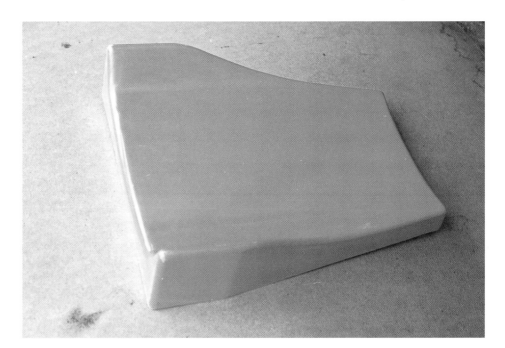

The purpose of this particular
component is to act as part of a
back-pack spray unit.

stronger. Obviously, these comparisons between sandwich-type and solid laminates will be affected by the thickness of each laminate, or amount of material they contain.

There is no easy way of controlling the thickness of a laminate, so the way to achieve a desired thickness is to use chopped strand matt of a weight that will laminate up to that thickness. Remember that the heavier the glass matt, the thicker it will be, and thick glass matt is difficult to laminate into tight corners and sharp detail. Therefore, don't consider using heavy matt until at least the third or fourth ply. What is heavy matt? A fairly heavy matt would be 600g/sq.m (2oz/sq.ft), while 900g/sq.m (3oz/sq.ft) is considered heavy.

When the thickness of the laminate has been decided, the material can be chosen to achieve that thickness or, as often happens, the nearest to the thickness that can be achieved with the chopped strand matt already held or most readily available. Another point to remember is that the lighter the chopped strand matt, the easier it will be to laminate, particularly in moulds of complex shape.

The spray unit in use.

Facing page

LAMINATING TIPS

A In tight corners, chopped strand matt has a tendency to bridge the angle.

B One method of preventing a void is to pre-fill the corner with strips of chopped strand matt. Applying progressively narrower strips will produce a shallow angle to fill.

C An alternative is to use long glass fibres to fill a tight corner and prevent a void forming.

D In a channel or similar recess, the chopped strand matt can bridge both corners, leaving two voids.

E In this case, strips of chopped strand matt that match the width of the channel can be used to prevent voids forming.

F When working with an open mould, it is essential that the wet laminate projects beyond the edges so that it can be trimmed back to the mould at the part-cured stage to provide a neat, clean edge.

G However, on vertical surfaces, the weight of the wet laminate can cause it to peel away from the mould face during the lay-up process.

H To prevent the wet laminate from peeling back, make sure that it extends by only a small amount beyond the mould edge, as shown.

As a guide to selecting chopped strand matt, material of 300g/sq.m (1oz/sq.ft) would, in theory, produce a finished thickness of 0.75mm (1⁄32in), but the strands will move about during laminating, especially if the shape is complex, and the thickness will vary slightly over the area being laminated. When several plies are used, the variation in thickness should be less. Matt of 450g/sq.m (1½oz/sq.ft) would give approximately 1mm (1⁄25in) thickness; 600g/sq.m (2oz/sq.ft) would give 1.5mm (1⁄16in); and 900g/sq.m (3oz/sq.ft) would give a little over 2mm (1⁄12in) thickness. The weights of chopped strand matt quoted here are widely available. If any other weight of chopped strand matt is purchased, it will be simple to calculate the approximate laminated thickness from the figures given.

Remember that many laminations are made from differing weights of glass matt, the lighter versions being used initially. Employing different weights of matt also enables you to select a combination that will result in the nearest to the planned component wall thickness.

If woven rovings or fabrics are to be used for all the plies in a laminate, or mixed with chopped strand matt, a little more thought will have to be given to calculating the thickness. For any given weight, woven glass materials produce a different thickness to chopped strand matt: for example, 600g/sq.m (2oz/sq.ft) chopped strand matt would give a thickness of 1.5mm (1⁄16in); 600g/sq.m (2oz/sq.ft) woven glass would produce a thickness of almost 3mm (1⁄8in). The reason for this is that there is little or no binder to hold the fibres together in a woven material, so there is nothing to be washed away by the resin, and binder does add bulk to the thickness of a fibre. Also, unlike the random arrangement of fibres in chopped strand matt, which move about during laminating, woven fibres are held in place during laminating by the weave itself. Make sure you allow for these differences when selecting materials for a specific thickness.

When using woven glass in a laminate made with polyester resin, remember that it should not be laminated directly on to more woven glass, as this would result in poor interlaminar strength, that is the bond between the plies would be weak. However, this problem can be overcome by putting a ply of chopped strand matt between each pair of woven plies. This would result in a well bound laminate, with extra stiffness as a result of using the woven glass. When considering the use of woven glass fabric, do not forget that it is more difficult to work with, particularly if the intended component has a lot of contours or sharp detail, although employing chopped strand in the same laminate will help to some degree, by helping to hold the woven material in place.

With the component wall thickness decided, the materials selected to achieve this thickness, and the mould prepared with release agent, work can begin on laminating of the first component.

First steps

The gel coat can be mixed and applied, remembering the points about the use of pigments or colouring pastes. Apply the coat in exactly the same way as when making the mould, taking care not to allow it to build up too much in the corners and areas of detail.

In most situations, one simple application of gel coat will give a satisfactory result, but when the component is to be self-coloured, it can be an advantage to double gel. This requires the application of one coat, which

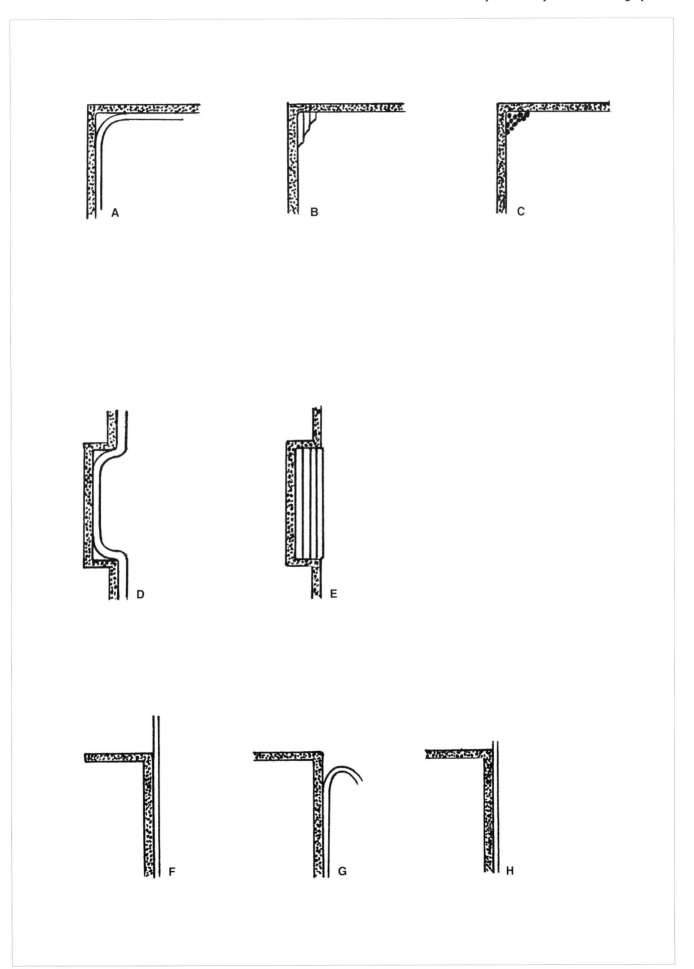

This mould has been gel coated and is awaiting lamination of the component.

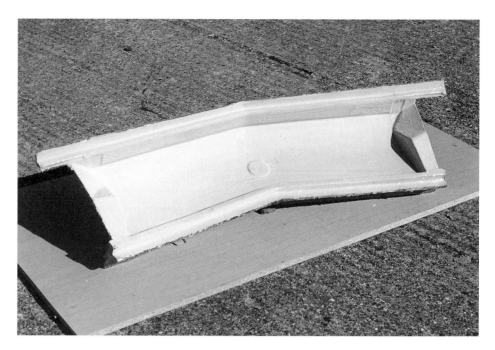

The pre-cut sections of chopped strand matt.

is allowed to reach an almost tack-free stage, followed by a second coat, pigmented and applied in exactly the same way as the first. The second coat provides extra depth to the colour and adds considerably to the gel coat thickness, permitting any mould join lines to be polished out without the fear of breaking through the gel coat. This also allows for further polishing at a later date, should any minor damage or scratches need attention. When the gel coat becomes almost tack-free, laminating can begin.

First, you must decide whether to make templates so that the glass matt can be cut to fit the mould. Some experienced laminators will tear the matt to approximate shape as they need each piece, but many also make templates and cut the matt to shape. When woven glass is to be used, it must be cut, as it is not possible to tear the material. The advantages of cutting the matt to shape are that it makes laminating easier and much quicker. Also, when more than one component is to be made, the material can be cut for more than one component at a time.

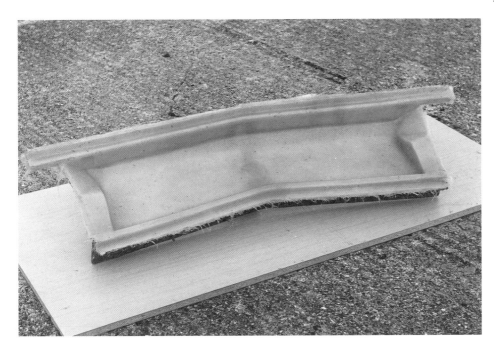

The completed lamination.

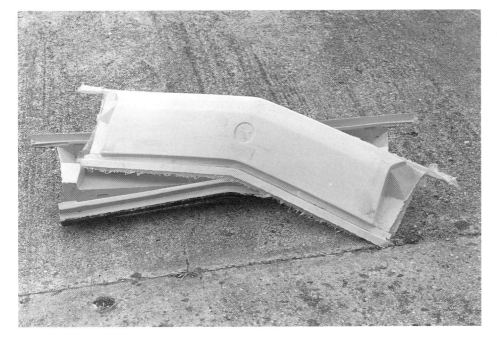

The cured laminated component after removal from the mould.

There are several ways of making templates, but the first task is to work out how many pieces will be needed to cover the surface of the mould. The shape of the component will be the major factor in making this decision, but in the case of very large areas, the material size must also be taken into account. It is not usually a good idea to attempt to cut the material into pieces of equal size; it is better to cut shapes to fit specific areas. If, for example, the proposed component was long with a bulbous shape at each end and maybe a deep channel running along the centre, it would be desirable to cut shapes to fit the bulbous ends, or it might be convenient to cut several small pieces to cover the shape, as these would be easier to laminate into place. Then strips wide enough to cover the interior of the channel section would be cut. There is no way that this book could give comprehensive guidance on how to decide upon the size and shape of the glass-fibre pieces needed for any given component lay-up, as each component will require substantially different sizes and shapes.

A typical hand lay-up in progress. Note that the dry chopped strand matt has been placed in the mould and is being wetted out.

With the mould in front of you, the ideal sizes and shapes will become more obvious.

When you have decided on the number of pieces and their approximate shapes, cut rough patterns from a suitable thin material that will follow the various contours of the mould. Some people employ paper as a pattern material, others use a fabric of some sort or woven glass. Whatever you choose, remember that it will not conform to a complex shape in the same manner as the resinated chopped strand matt. However, this is not a problem, as there will be overlaps in the glass matt when the lamination is carried out, and any discrepancies in the pattern shapes can be lost in those overlaps, as these need not be uniform. Hold each roughly shaped piece in place in the mould and mark it to a more accurate shape, then remove it and trim it to size. It is always a good idea to check the fit of each piece in the mould again, making any further adjustments to its shape as necessary.

Lay the patterns on the glass matt or woven glass, and cut around them with a sharp knife. Make sure you cut enough pieces to complete the lamination before mixing any resin, so that you will not be cutting matt with resin covered hands.

How much resin?

When you are ready to begin laminating, you will need to give some thought to the amount of resin to mix. The points to consider are the size of the mould and whether the entire surface can be covered with one ply in one mix or, if not, how much of the mould can be laminated with each resin mix. If the mould is very large, don't try to laminate too much in one go, as the resin may start to arc (gel) before you have consolidated the area fully. Similarly, if the mould is of complex shape with return flanges and other detail, it will take longer to laminate than a simple shape. Other features to consider are the catalyst-to-resin ratio (1-2%), the speed of the

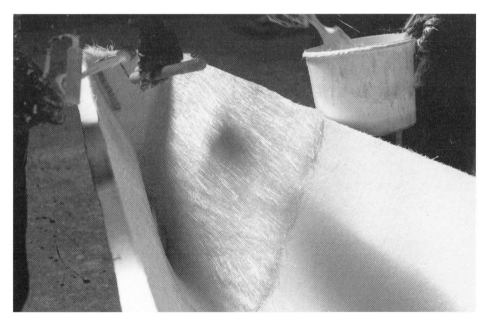

Above left **A boat mould ready for use.**

Above **Gel coat being applied to the boat mould.**

Left **The first ply of chopped strand matt being applied to the boat mould.**

catalyst and, as always, the atmospheric conditions prevailing at the time, which will affect the pot life of the mixed resin. The final consideration is the laminator's ability: a person with some laminating experience will always be quicker than a beginner.

The pot life of a resin mix can be shortened or lengthened by varying the amount of catalyst used and, thus, speeding up or slowing down the rate of cure. It can also be greatly extended by the type of catalyst chosen, that is high-, medium- or low-activity. Experienced laminators will know which to use to suit the prevailing conditions, but beginners should avoid high-activity catalysts. Low-activity catalysts are normally employed when very large moulds are being used, or when very thick laminates are to be made. Another important use for low-activity catalysts is when the working temperature is high and the minimum amount of a higher-activity

Above **After the first glass ply has been wetted out with resin, a roller is used to consolidate it.**

Above right **The completed lamination for the required hull thickness. Note the slot along the bottom.**

catalyst would still result in too short a pot life. Remember, the ratio of catalyst to resin should never fall below 1%, so although the pot life of a resin mix can be adjusted by the amount of catalyst added, the minimum quantity must still be added to effect the full arc of the resin. For obvious reasons, exceeding the recommended upper ratio level could be disastrous, as the resin mix could suddenly arc in the middle of laminating.

Most normal bonding is carried out with general-purpose resin and medium-activity catalyst, and the pot life controlled by varying the mixing ratio. With these materials, the pot life can be made to range from approximately ten minutes to an hour. Where the working temperature is likely to be higher than 21°C (70°F), or if the component is particularly large, a low-activity catalyst would be preferable.

It is important to remember that the resin has a pot life. To avoid this becoming a problem when you begin laminating, only wet out an area of glass matt that you can consolidate in a few minutes, using the roller and stippling action with a paint brush. Then proceed to another small area. After a while, you will be able to gauge the approximate time that the resin remains usable, and then you can begin to wet out larger areas at a time. The advantage of wetting out only a small area is that if the resin shows signs of gelling, that is it begins to thicken, you will be able to consolidate the area before the resin gels completely, which is crucial. No matter how large or small an area, even though it may only cover part of the mould's surface, it must be consolidated fully. Then you can simply mix more resin and carry on. Although the area just consolidated will be in what is called a 'green' state, that is part cured, it will combine very well with the next area you laminate. In fact, even if the previously consolidated area was well cured, it would still be possible to complete the component, and the bond at the overlaps between sections would still be satisfactory.

However, you should always wet out as much area and consolidate in one go as safely possible, then proceed with the remainder as soon as you can, except when part of a component is to be laminated and deliberately left to cure before continuing with the remainder. An example of this situation is where the mould shape includes an overhang, that is a return flange. If glass is applied to this at the same time as the rest of the mould, the wet laminate will tend to fall away from the underside of the flange, and you will find great difficulty in making it stay put. Sometimes, tilting the mould so that the overhang is at a less severe angle will help, but in some cases, a much better solution is to stand the mould on its side and laminate the flange only, allowing this to achieve a part cure before placing the mould in a suitable position for laminating the remainder of the component. Alternatively, you could laminate the main area first, allow it to part cure, then tilt the mould and laminate the flange. This method of laminating only part of a component at a time can also be used for any other difficult areas.

Above left **The completed lamination of the boat hull. Note that the slot in the bottom now has a vertical wooden member in it, which has been laminated over to form a longitudinal stiffener. This would have been carried out as a second operation, after the main lamination had been allowed to cure, to prevent distortion.**

Above **The completed boat hull being removed from the mould.**

Laminating

The resin should be mixed in the same way as when making the mould. Brush a generous coat over the area to be laminated and lay a piece of chopped strand matt over this area. If different weights of chopped strand matt are being laminated, remember to use the lighter-weight matt for the first ply. Work the glass matt into the resin with the consolidating roller, which will bring the resin up through the matt and it will begin to be wetted out. However, it is unlikely that there will be enough resin to completely wet out the matt, which is essential, so add more resin with a suitable size of paint brush. When using a brush to apply resin, employ the stippling action described previously, which will push the resin well into the matt

A completed laminate on a male mould, which will ensure a good finish on the inside of the component.

and help force air out of the lamination. Moreover, the dabbing action does not move the random fibres of the glass matt as much as a brushing action. If the fibres become displaced too much, this can result in thin areas within the finished laminate, although when several plies are being laminated this should not be a major problem. When the matt is fully wetted, leave it for a short while to allow the resin to soak the binder off the glass fibres. It is not possible to specify a time for this, as the rate at which the binder is dissolved will depend on the make of matt and the type of binder. As a rule, it should take less than a minute, but do not rely on time, rather go by the visual appearance. The matt will take on a saturated translucent appearance, indicating that it is fully wetted out.

At this point, use the consolidating roller to compress the matt on to the mould surface. There are no set rules governing the direction or sequence of rolling, but you must ensure that every part of the matt is covered. Where there is sharp detail or any area where you cannot use the roller effectively, compress the matt with a brush by stippling. This part of the process ensures that the glass matt is in close contact with the mould surface, and that no air is trapped in or under the matt. As the matt is compressed, you will see that the air is being removed, while the resin will change from a milky white to an almost transparent appearance. Any remaining bubbles of trapped air will almost always be visible and can be dealt with by dabbing with the brush, which should force the air out through the matt.

When the first area of the lamination has reached this stage, repeat the process for the next area, or the remainder of the mould, unless the entire mould has been covered in one go. Add the second ply in the same manner. If the mould is being laminated in sections, it is a good idea to move the overlaps of the sections slightly to prevent prominent ridges from forming.

There is no need to wait for any of the plies to part cure, unless the laminate thickness is likely to exceed approximately 4mm (⅙in). Then it is advisable to allow the first two or three plies to cure prior to laminating the remainder. The reason for this is to prevent an exotherm caused by the

A deep version of a fan duct
made on a split male mould.

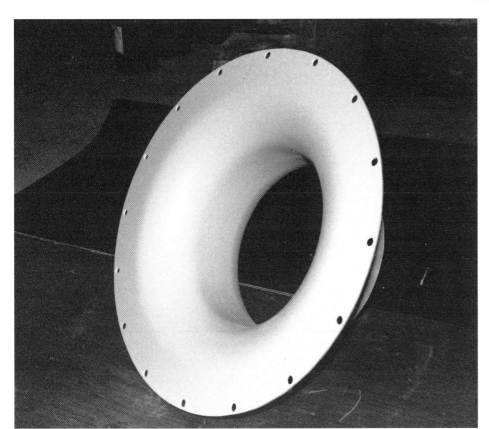

GRP laminating is ideal for
making forms such as this
satellite dish.

build up of excessive heat as the resin cures. The foregoing assumes that the matt has a weight of not more than 600g/sq.m (2oz/sq.ft). If the matt is heavier than this, restrict the number of plies to two, although it is unlikely that very heavy glass matt would be used for the first few plies. Also, when very heavy matt is being used, or an extra thick laminate is planned, a lower-activity catalyst should be employed to prevent too fast a cure and the resultant temperature rise.

Most normal GRP components, such as car bodywork, motor cycle fairings, small boat hulls, etc, will have wall thicknesses of between 3 and 5mm (⅛ and ⅕in), and the weights of matt required can be easily calculated by assuming that 400g/sq.m (1¼oz/sq.ft) will produce a 1mm (¹⁄₂₅in) thick laminate. If the proposed component is likely to have a wall thickness far in excess of these normal applications, heavier matt would be utilized and the previously mentioned points taken into account.

We will assume that the required number of plies are in place over the entire mould, but that the cure has not taken place. During the laminating process, you may have discovered some areas where the glass matt was reluctant to stay in place—a tight corner perhaps, or some sharp detail—which would result in voids. One way to hold the matt tightly in these areas is to make a final lamination over them with a ply, or even two plies, of glass tissue.

Final cure

With the laminate fully consolidated, and any difficult areas covered with a ply or two of tissue, all that is left at this stage is to allow a full cure to take place. When the laminate has reached the green stage (indicated by the resin having the texture of hard rubber), the excess laminate that protrudes over the edge of the mould can be trimmed off with a sharp knife. This gets rid of sharp and potentially dangerous laminate prior to removing the component from the mould, and it also means that less trimming of the component will be required when it has been removed. Under most normal conditions, the laminate will appear to be cured after one or two hours, but it should be left for at least 36 hours before attempting to remove it from the mould. If the component is large, or if it has a complex shape, it may take more effort to remove from the mould. If this is the case, it should be left in the mould for three or four days before attempting removal.

Removal from the mould

If the mould is a sectional type, removing the component may be much easier than if it is in one piece. In the former case, begin by removing the bolts that hold the mould sections together, then tap thin tapered wedges between the joining flanges, spacing them 125-150mm (5-6in) apart. The wedges can be made from a variety of materials, such as aluminium, plastic or hard wood. To begin with, tap the wedges in to a depth of 15-18mm (⅝-¾in). If the mould has a thick wall and is very stiff, the wedges will often release the mould very easily. A sign that this is occurring—apart from a gap beginning to form between the sections—is a cracking sound as the mould separates from the component.

If the wedges have been tapped in as described, but there is no apparent separation of mould from component, leave the wedges in place and

GRP laminates are widely used for industrial applications. This roof panel is a typical example. Complete roof sections simulating tiles or slates are produced, together with panels imitating stone- and brickwork.

Many forms of equipment covers and cases can be made in GRP. This is an example of a three-piece case.

This large GRP emblem was made for the front of Highbury Stadium, the home of the Arsenal football team.

Above GRP is widely used for automotive applications. In this case, a set of panels has been made to transform the appearance of the Fiat X/19 sports car shown.

Right The GRP rear spoiler for the X/19.

Right This replacement front panel for a car is a typical application for GRP.

work around the mould with a hard rubber mallet, delivering several sharp blows. This has the effect of producing a shock wave, and the resultant vibration is often successful in causing the separation of mould and component. Sometimes, however, more effort will be needed. If so, tap the wedges in a little further and, if necessary, use the rubber mallet again. Take care when doing this, as you may cause damage to the mould or component, or both.

If the mould is a one-piece version, the approach to component removal will be different. Since there will be no mould split lines to separate, you will have to work on the component itself, and as the wall thickness will be much less than the mould, you must take care to prevent any damage from occurring.

If the component has a return flange around its edge, that is the lamination extends beyond the area of the mould on to its edge flange, you can begin removing the component by inserting thin wedges under the flange, 125-150mm (5-6in) apart. If this does not begin to remove the component, give the mould some sharp blows with a rubber mallet, particularly in the areas furthest from the edge. If no movement of the component has occurred, use a blunt lever of some kind to gently prise the flange upwards. If some movement takes place, tap the wedges in a little further and continue to lever gently at various points around the edge of the mould. A combination of force from the wedges, the mallet blows and careful leverage should free the component from the mould.

If the mould is a one-piece type and the component does not extend on to an external flange, the removal process will be slightly different. In this case, use the rubber mallet to deliver a series of sharp blows over the entire mould. These should be firm, but not too hard, otherwise cracks will appear in the gel coated surface of the mould. The next stage is to ease the edges of the component away from the mould wall. To do this, gently push a blunt instrument, such as a round-tipped pallet knife, between the mould and component, but be careful, especially if the component is curved, as a flat blade will damage the surface. To prevent this type of damage, only employ a metallic instrument to start the separation of the component from the mould, then use strips of some other material, such as wood or, better still, rigid plastic. The width of these strips is not critical,

This set of vintage-style sports car wings is another typical automotive application for GRP.

but do not make them very wide if the component has a deeply curved surface. The advantage of using plastic for these strips is that it will tend to bend to the shape of the component without causing damage. Push the strips down between the component and mould, starting in the middle of a long edge, which is likely to be the most flexible part, as this will be the easiest spot to insert the first strips. Once the component begins to separate from the mould, it will become easier to insert more strips. Tap or push gently until they will go no further, listening for the cracking sound of separation. In some cases, where small components are concerned, once some edge separation has taken place, the component can be carefully pulled from the mould with pincers.

In addition to these methods of removing a component from its mould, compressed air can be employed. If air attachments have been laminated in, or holes left and plugged, use them to blow compressed air in as a means of forcing a separation between the mould and component. Although compressed air is not widely used by professional laminators, it is extremely useful when dealing with very complex components.

The removal of a GRP component from its mould may be very easy or sometimes difficult. However, by using the tips given here, together with some common sense and patience, you should be able to release the component without too much trouble, provided there are no undercuts and the release preparation of the mould has been carried out correctly.

Final detailing

All that remains is to trim the component. If it has been wet trimmed, that is excess laminate removed with a knife at the green state, final trimming will be easy. In some cases, the edges will simply need sanding by hand with a medium or coarse grade of abrasive sheet, or this can be done with an electric angle sander. Any holes should be drilled undersize and opened out with a rotary file or hand file, which will produce cleaner edges.

If any attachments, such as metal inserts or brackets are required, they should be bonded in using a two-part epoxy adhesive, of the type that is available from most hardware stores. The same adhesive can be used to join other moulded parts to the main lamination after it has been removed from the mould if these would have made the shape too difficult to mould in one piece. Another way of adding these separate pieces of the component is to use normal polyester body filler. This will stick the parts in place and, at the same time, can be utilized to blend out any join lines between the parts.

If the moulded component has a coloured gel coat surface and is to be used without any other finish, it may have visible mould join lines. The best way of removing these is to pare them down to the moulded surface with a sharp scraper or a wood chisel, held at right angles to the surface. When any flash has been removed, and the join line made to match the contours of the component, the area can be polished with cutting compound (normally used for polishing newly sprayed paint) to match the remainder of the component. Either polish the finish by hand, or use a lamb's-wool or similar polishing mop in an electric drill. Both methods will produce an excellent finish that matches the rest of the component.

These notes simply cover the lamination of a GRP component with poly ester resin and chopped strand matt. While it would be impossible to give detailed instructions that would cover every possible application, the information provided will be applicable to most normal laminating requirements and situations.

Using a vinylester resin

If, instead of polyester, a vinylester resin is chosen for the lamination (to achieve a tougher component or one with better high-temperature performance), the laminating technique will be the same, but more attention will have to be paid to the resin itself. Vinylester resin systems are usually unaccelerated, which produces a longer storage life, but does mean that an accelerator must be added at the same time as the catalyst.

Left **The marine industry is a major user of GRP, employing the material to construct all manner of vessels from small dinghys to large boats and even small ships. This is a prime example, both the hull and upper superstructure being formed from GRP mouldings.**

Below left **Another typical marine application for GRP.**

Below **A moulded GRP dinghy.**

There are many suppliers of vinylester resin systems, which vary from one supplier to another, making it impossible to give mixing ratio details. The reason for the many variants is that vinylesters lend themselves to being modified to give excellent corrosion resistance to a wide range of chemicals, including some strong alkalis, acids and many industrial solvents. In fact, the range of chemicals to which vinylesters are resistant is almost endless. Many of these resin systems are used in the manufacture of chemical processing equipment, such as mixing vessels, pipes, storage tanks, ducting, etc. Different chemicals will require different modifications to the resin, and there can't be one resin that is resistant to all chemicals. Therefore, some manufacturers will have several variants, and each variant will have specific processing details, including the type and amount of accelerator and catalyst.

As can be seen, vinylesters have great potential, but because of the number of possible variants, it is important to consult the supplier to establish the correct version for the proposed application, together with the relevant processing details. The laminating process will be virtually the same as for a polyester system, and the differences, if any, are most likely to be

Below **GRP is an excellent material for constructing large storage vessels. This underground storage tank was made by the wet lay-up method.**

Below right **A GRP moulding after removal from the mould. Note the 'flash' formed by the joints in the mould. This will be sanded off before the component is fitted out with the electronics it will contain.**

in the resin pot life, gel time or cure time. The data sheet for the selected resin will give this information.

If a gel coat is required when utilizing vinylester resin, you can use a normal polyester version, which will work very well. It would be incorrect to say that vinylester gels are not available, as some manufacturers supply them as tooling gels for moulds to give surfaces a high degree of scratch resistance and good wear properties. This type of gel is not normally used on moulded components, however, as its hardness can lead to cracking. Again, your supplier will be able to advise you on what is available and its suitability.

The method for removing a vinylester component from the mould is the same as that for polyesters, as are the trimming and finishing processes.

This chapter has described the basic techniques for laminating with polyester and vinylester resins. The great potential offered by these materials should be within the grasp of most people wishing to take advantage of them, but like all crafts, there is a learning curve, and part of that is adapting or finding methods that suit you and your equipment.

An unusual application for GRP: leather-effect panels for desk tops, etc. Real leather was used as a pattern, and with only one ply of chopped-strand matt, the resulting panel is quite flexible.

GRP has been widely used for many types of furniture. This combined table and seats for a restaurant is a prime example.

6

Epoxy laminating by hand

Although woven glass fabrics and unidirectional glass fibres are widely used in wet lay-up with polyester resin, considerably improving mechanical performance, when they are utilized with epoxy resin systems, much higher structural performance can be achieved. There are two basic reasons for this. One is that the excellent adhesive qualities of epoxy resin systems designed for wet laminating offer better interlaminar strength, that is the bonding of one ply to the next. The other is that the epoxy results in a much tougher matrix, depending on the resin content of the laminate.

The techniques for laminating with epoxy resins are very different from those required for polyester wet lay-up and, often, additional equipment is required, such as a vacuum pump, vacuum bags and sealing materials. Moreover, epoxy resins are far more expensive than polyesters.

Because of the much better structural performance offered by the combination of epoxy resin and woven fabrics, components can be made thinner and, therefore, much lighter. The chemical nature of the curing process results in a much more stable laminate which, when fully cured, will maintain its structural performance. This means that if mechanical tests were carried out immediately after a component was fully cured (for such aspects as beam shear stiffness, or any other relevant mechanical performance requirement), then repeated some years later, there would be very little difference between the two sets of test results. Components made with polyester would not maintain their mechanical performance in the same way. Where the structural performance of a laminate is being relied upon, it is important that the performance is maintained, and in this situation, an epoxy resin system is ideal. The excellent mechanical performance, resultant toughness and chemical stability make components made with epoxy very durable.

The same type of mould can be used and, in most cases, moulds made for polyester laminating can also be used with epoxy resins. The release treatment applied to the mould prior to laminating can be exactly the same as well. However, when epoxy resin systems are being utilized, it is common for liquid release agents to be used, some of which are available in aerosol spray cans. These spray releases work very well, and they have a long shelf life, whereas liquid release agents for brush or pad application can become contaminated by humidity and may fail to work.

Normally, no gel coat is used with an epoxy resin system, and gels formulated specifically for epoxy resin are rarely available, although they are not unknown. If an epoxy gel is obtained, follow the supplier's advice for the mixing ratio. As with a polyester gel, it is applied by brush and allowed to become almost tack-free before proceeding with the laminating stage. In the absence of an epoxy gel coat, some laminators will use a polyester gel coat. Although considered wrong, it does work. In this case, the gel coat should be left to a much more advanced stage of cure before laminating on to it with the epoxy. The better adhesive properties of the epoxy will ensure a good bond between the cured polyester gel coat and the following laminate. However, the use of polyester gel coats on epoxy components intended for structural use is not recommended. This is due to the differing mechanical performance of the two resin systems.

Suitable reinforcement

In any event, gel coats are not so important when laminating with epoxy resins. One reason for this is that the glass reinforcement used is always woven fabric or some type of unidirectional fibre, and these do not tend to show through the component's surface to the same degree as chopped strand matt does with polyester when there is little or no gel coat. Another reason that epoxy laminated components with no gel still have a good external finish is that the lamination is consolidated under pressure.

As explained previously, there is a wide range of woven glass fabrics, and each has its particular advantages. For example, plain weave will give a component more stiffness than the same weight of a complicated weave, but the latter will often be more drapable, that is it will be easier to lay over a complicated shape during laminating. The most difficult material to use in components with significant contours are unidirectional fibres, but they give the greatest stiffness for a given weight of glass. If the component is flat or has very gentle contours, laminating with unidirectional fibres will be as easy as with any other glass reinforcement.

It is common to employ more than one type of glass reinforcement in the same component. For example, if the item has a complex shape, a weave that is more drapable should be used over the entire surface of the mould, and extra stiffness added where needed by laying in unidirectional fibres at these points. It must be remembered that unidirectional fibres will give great stiffness along the fibre direction, but nothing across it. Therefore, where unidirectional material is to be used on its own, some of the plies in the laminate must be laid at right angles to the others, ensuring that mechanical performance is achieved in both directions.

Another advantage of using epoxy resin is that several plies of woven glass fabric can be laminated directly on top of each other, and the adhesive qualities of the epoxy resin will ensure a far better interlaminar performance than can be achieved with polyester resin. The wall thickness of a component made completely with woven fabric will be constant, since the glass fibres do not move about in the same way as in chopped strand matt, the nature of the weave holding the fibres in place. Moreover, woven fabrics do not rely on a binder to hold the fibres together, so there is little or no change in the fibres' bulk or thickness when laminating. This aids calculating the amount of the selected weave that will be required to achieve the desired component wall thickness. It is important to remember that woven glass does not reduce in thickness when wet laminating as much as chopped strand matt, which means that fewer woven plies will be required to achieve the same thickness.

In the case of woven fabrics, it is always advisable to cut the material to size and shape prior to starting the lamination. Woven fabrics cannot be torn by hand in the same manner as chopped strand matt and, because of the lack of binder, they are not so stiff in the dry state. Therefore, they are not so easy to cut once in position in the mould. A major advantage of woven fabrics is that the weave holds the material together, which means that very accurate shapes can be cut without fear of the material falling apart. This can be useful, especially when the component is of a complex shape. It also allows you to control the overlaps, both in size and location.

Unidirectional fibres are normally stitched together with a fine thread, as there are no cross fibres to hold them together, and a little more care is needed when cutting them to shape. It is unlikely that you will need to cut complex shapes from stitched unidirectional fibres, as they are usually employed on large areas with shallow contours to add stiffness. A complex shape will have inherent stiffness and is unlikely to need reinforcement with this material.

Because woven fabrics can be cut to neat accurate shapes, it is worth taking the time to make cutting templates. Thin closely woven glass cloth can be used for patterns, or tissue paper, or anything that can be made to follow closely the contours of the mould. Mark the outline of each shape, allowing for any folds in the pattern material, cut it out and try it back in the mould, trimming if necessary. Repeat the process until you have covered the mould with conveniently shaped patterns. Then transfer the shapes to a more rigid material. If you are only making a one-off, or a very small number of components, stout card would do, but if you intend making more components, or if the lamination will have a considerable number of plies, it is advisable to make the templates from something more solid, such as plywood, fibre board or aluminium. Remember, you will be cutting around these templates with a sharp knife, so they must be able to withstand the occasional slip with the blade.

Beginning the lamination

Epoxy resin mixing ratios will vary considerably from one manufacturer to another. Be sure to check the data sheet for the correct ratio of resin (part A) to hardener (part B). Note that in most cases with epoxy resin instructions, you add a hardener not a catalyst, and this is usually referred to as part B. The ratio may be by weight or volume, but in some cases, it must be by weight only. A small battery powered letter balance is ideal for weighing out the required amounts for mixes of up to 2kg (4½lb). For ratios by volume, any pre-calibrated vessels will do, or simply make your own by marking suitable plastic bottles.

When the correct ratio of resin to hardener has been measured out, you can mix them by hand. When extra large batches of resin are required, an electric mixer may be used, but for most applications, hand mixing is satisfactory.

The pot life of the resin mix will depend mainly on the speed of the hardener. Many manufacturers of epoxy resin systems offer fast, medium and slow hardeners, which produce variations in pot life from minutes to hours. The selection of hardener will depend on the job in hand: if this is large or particularly complicated, and the lamination will take a long time to complete, a slow hardener must be used. If, on the other hand, the component is small and simple, or the aim is to repeat the process as quickly as possible, a fast hardener should be selected. The pot life will also be affected by the amount in the mix and the working temperature.

If the mix is rather large, or the temperature very high, it is a good idea to pour the mixed resin into some form of shallow tray, thus reducing its bulk. This will help extend the pot life. When some experience has been gained with a resin system, it is possible to mix slow and rapid hardeners to achieve a pot life that gives time to complete the laminate, but initiates a cure shortly after. Epoxy resin systems are not as sensitive to hardener ratio as polyesters, but it is not a good idea to add excess hardener in an attempt to speed up the cure. If the manufacturer's recommended ratios are exceeded, the structural or mechanical performance of the cured laminate may be reduced. This is because the extra hardener will upset the chemical balance that ensures optimum performance. If speed is important, use a fast hardener.

When wet laminating with epoxy resin systems, there are two different methods of wetting out the glass fabric. One is to put the dry fabric into place in the mould, then brush on the resin. Since the laminate will be cured under pressure, some laminators maintain that it is unnecessary to brush resin on to the mould first, but brushing a coat of resin over the mould serves two purposes: it ensures that the mould surface is fully wetted, which is important to a good finish, and it helps to hold the glass fabric in place while the remaining resin is applied.

With the fabric in place, the resin can be worked in with a paint brush. Woven fabric allows a normal brushing action to be employed; the stippling process used on chopped strand matt is not so critical on woven fabric, as the fibres do not move about so freely. However, stippling the resin can help if the weave of the fabric is particularly fine or tight. The important aspect is to ensure that the woven fabric is completely wetted out, but not flooded, otherwise the laminate will be resin rich, and this will reduce its performance. When laminating woven glass fabric with epoxy resin, there is no need to utilize a roller, as with chopped strand matt, nor is there any need to wait for a binder on the glass to dissolve. Therefore, as soon as the first ply has been wetted out, the second ply can be added, and so on until the required number of plies is in place.

The second method of wetting out the glass fabric is carried out before putting it in the mould. Simply lay the pieces of fabric on a sheet of polythene and wet out with a brush, as before. Then carefully peel the wet fabric from the polythene and lay it in the mould. Alternatively, transfer the wetted glass fabric into the mould on the polythene, using the clean side of the polythene to manipulate the fabric into place. Peel the polythene off the fabric, and use the brush to make any final adjustments to its position.

If the component is of a structural nature, wetting out the fabric on polythene will allow you to optimize the performance of the laminate with a more accurate resin-to-glass ratio. This can be achieved by wetting out the fabric, then going over it with a plastic blade of some kind to squeeze out excess resin. Use light pressure on the blade and work the resin out to and off the edges of the fabric shape. To obtain an exact resin-to-glass ratio, measure the area of the glass, then weigh out the correct amount of resin for this area. Using the same type of plastic blade or scraper, comb the resin into the fabric, moving it about until the area has been wetted out completely. However, this method can be tedious or difficult, especially if the fabric has been cut into odd shapes to fit the mould.

Wetting out the glass on polythene can be advantageous when the fabric must be cut into complex shapes and has a loose weave that tends to fall apart or be dragged out of shape as it is cut. In this situation, the fabric will often be easier to cut when wet, so some laminators wet out an uncut section, then lay a second sheet of polythene on top of the wet resin before cutting out the required shapes. Because the wet resin is between two sheets of polythene, the cutting templates can be used for the required shapes. Finally, one layer of polythene is removed and the glass transferred to the mould.

Whichever method you choose for wetting out the glass fabric, the result will be the same. Remember, however, that for woven glass, the amount of resin to glass will be very different to that required for chopped strand matt. There will be minor differences depending on the type of weave and the weight, but as a guide, the amount of resin should be 1-1¼ times the weight of glass to produce a satisfactory finished laminate. If the optimum resin-to-glass ratio is needed for maximum structural performance, it is advisable to consult the suppliers of the glass and resin, at the time of purchase, due to the very wide selection of fabric types and considerable number of resin manufacturers, all of whom have their own formulations and performance data.

Newcomers to laminating with epoxy resin should not worry too much about achieving the perfect resin-to-glass ratio, as ultimate structural performance is rarely sought through the wet lay-up method. The guide given earlier will produce a satisfactory result for most applications.

Preparing for vacuum

With all the plies of glass in the mould and wetted out, the next stage is to prepare the lamination for the application of vacuum, which will provide the consolidating pressure during the cure. Therefore, it is essential that the lamination is under vacuum pressure before the resin begins to gel, which is the first stage of the cure.

The first task is to cover the wetted out fabric with a release membrane. This is a purpose-made self-releasing plastic film. Being very thin, it can be made to follow the contours of the component relatively easily, but since it is a flat sheet, it won't actually form to compound shapes. However, the material is thin enough that any small folds will not cause problems, and on complex shapes, it is normal to cut the film into pieces so that it can be tailored into the mould, reducing the number of folds.

The release membrane material can also be purchased with very tiny perforations, which allow the air to escape when the vacuum is applied. However, unless the component being made is very large, vacuum pressure can be applied successfully without the need for this perforated film. The air can escape through the overlaps if the membrane is put into the mould in pieces. Another purpose of the perforations is to allow any excess resin to bleed through them when pressure is applied.

The next part of the process is to line the mould with an air bleed layer. This soft felt-like material can be purchased in a range of thicknesses, the thicker versions being suitable for large moulds with no intricate detail. It should be laid in the mould, on top of the release film. Again, it can be cut into conveniently shaped pieces, and held in place with tabs of masking tape. The main purpose of the air bleed layer is to allow the air to be drawn off by the vacuum pump, its porosity providing an easy passage for the air. When perforated release film is used, the air bleed layer also soaks up any excess resin forced out through the perforations.

With the air bleed layer in place, all that remains is to cover the entire lamination with vacuum-bag material. This purpose-made plastic sheeting comes in roll form. Some laminators use commercial polythene instead, which is much cheaper, and while this will work, it is not as airtight as the purpose-made material. When using ordinary polythene, it is essential to keep the vacuum pump running throughout the cure.

Prior to putting the vacuum-bag material in place, sealing tape must be stuck to the flange around the edge of the mould. This will hold the material in place. Again, it is purpose-made and takes the form of an extruded mastic, which is about 10mm (⅜in) wide and supplied in rolls on a release paper. A similar product is made for sealing double-glazed windows, and this works very well at ambient temperatures. The purpose-made tape, however, must be used for curing resins at elevated temperatures.

Although the vacuum-bag material is thin, it will not form to compound shapes and, while it does possess a degree of elasticity, it is not intended to be stretched over the mould. Therefore, the vacuum bag must be made very slack by cutting it much larger than the area it is to cover. To make the sheet material fit a compound shape, you will need to form many folds, but this doesn't matter as long as they are all sealed.

This method of making a vacuum bag should be used regardless of the shape of the mould, but to simplify the description of the technique, we will assume that the mould is rectangular in shape and female in form. The piece of vacuum bag material needed should measure the dimensions of the base of the mould in length and width, with double the depth of the mould added to both dimensions, plus approximately another 20%. The latter will provide a margin for forming the seal and ensure a slack bag.

Before putting the vacuum-bag material into the mould, check that the sealing tape is in position—approximately in the centre of the mould flange—and that it is pressed down well by running your thumb along the backing paper. Leave the paper on the tape at this stage, otherwise the bag will keep sticking to it as you position the material. Place the material over the mould, then start on one long side by peeling back 300-475mm (12-18in) of the backing paper and positioning the bag material so that it overlaps the tape by about 25mm (1in). Press it down on to the tape, which will help hold the material in place. Work along the tape, carefully peeling off the backing paper and pressing the bag material into place by running your thumb along it. Approximately half-way along the side of the mould, form a small tuck. To do this, you will need a short length of sealing tape. With a fairly large mould, this should be 50-75mm (2-3in) long, but there are no set rules governing the size of tucks. Take the piece of sealing tape and stick one end to the tape that runs around the mould so that it projects vertically upwards. Then stick the bag material up one side of the vertical tape, over the end and down the other side. Continue sticking down the bag material along the side of the mould until you reach the corner. At this point, you should form another tuck in the same manner as before. The length of this corner tuck will be governed by the amount of

A mould with lay-up in place and a flat-sheet vacuum bag applied. Note the tucks formed with the sealing tape on the mould flange and where the folds in the vacuum bag are made to form in the corner of the mould. There will be many small creases over the surface

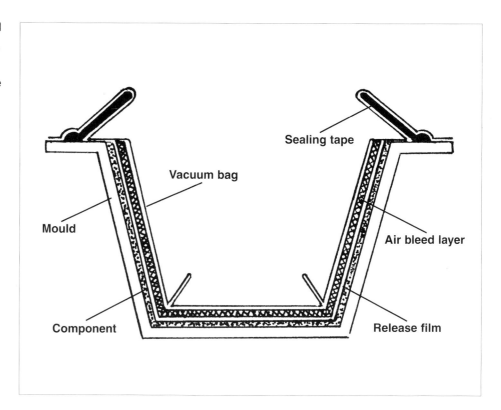

bag material that needs taking up as a result of turning the corner, bearing in mind that the edge of the bag along the width of the mould should also project beyond the sealing tape by about 25mm (1in). Continue in this way around the remainder of the mould, making a tuck at each corner and another at the centre of each side.

Before completing the bag seal, you must add a vacuum outlet, and there is a variety of commercially-made units to choose from. To fit the outlet, a small hole must be made in the bag. The vacuum take-off (a tube containing a one-way valve), which has a large circular base, is passed through the hole from inside the bag, and a clamping ring is screwed on from the outside. This sandwiches the bag material and is normally sealed by some form of gasket. With large moulds, or moulds that are to be used repeatedly, a vacuum take-off can be laminated into the mould itself, or bonded in later.

A simpler and cheaper way of forming a vacuum outlet is to seal the vacuum pipe itself into the edge of the bag. This is made possible by the fact that the pipe is usually reinforced and of comparatively small diameter. To form the seal, wrap a piece of sealing tape around the pipe 50-75mm (2-3in) from the end, but before taking the backing paper off the tape, attach a 175-200mm (7-8in) long piece of porous air bleed material to the end of the pipe, rolling it to form an extension to the pipe and securing it with masking tape. This will prevent the vacuum bag from being sucked over the end of the pipe, and will form a direct airway from the air bleed layer to the pipe. Pull a short length of the bag material off the seal and pass the pipe through. Having removed the backing paper from the sealing tape on the pipe, seal the bag around the pipe and back down on to the mould flange. Make sure that the air bleed material around the pipe rests on the air bleed layer in the mould.

Some laminators prefer to use a short length of small-diameter metal pipe to seal into the vacuum bag so that the vacuum pipe can be pushed

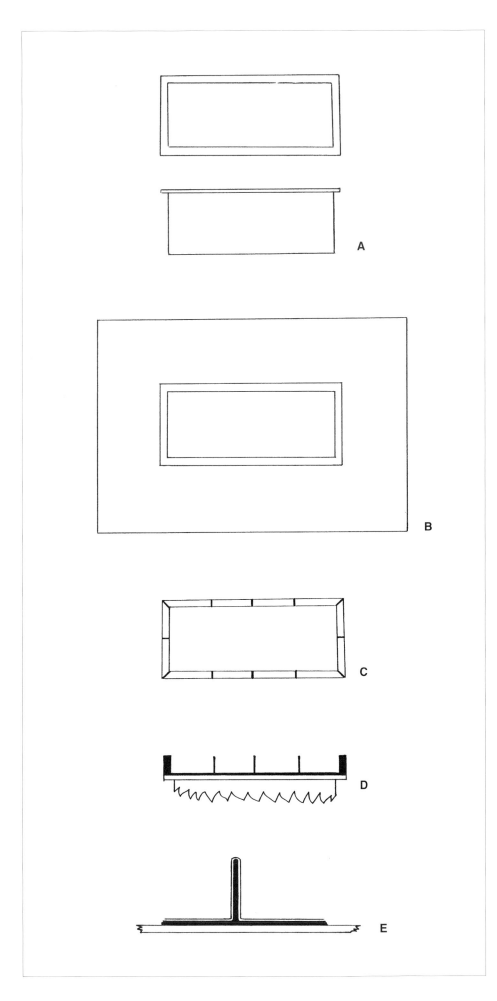

FITTING A VACUUM BAG

A Plan and side view of a typical rectangular mould.

B Plan view of the flat sheet vacuum-bag material cut to size, which is the length of the mould plus twice the depth plus approximately 20%. Use the same formula when calculating the width.

C Plan view of the mould and the positions of the intended tucks in the vacuum bag.

D Side view of the mould with the tucks in the vacuum bag formed. Those at the corners only seem wider because they are seen from an angle and not edge on.

E An individual tuck formed in the vacuum bag. Shown is a side view of the mould flange with the vacuum bag material stuck to the flange and around the vertical tab of sealing tape, which has been added to that running around the flange of the mould. This serves to take up the excess vacuum bag material needed to obtain the depth and shape of the mould. This basic principle of vacuum bag manufacture, although looking untidy, can be utilized on almost any mould. Where the mould is larger than the available vacuum bag material, simply join the material with overlapping joints secured with sealing tape.

VACUUM OUTLETS

A A purpose-made vacuum
outlet with built-in shut-off
valve, which maintains the
vacuum when the pump is
disconnected, provided there
are no leaks in the bag. This
allows a mould to be moved
without taking the pump with it.
This type of outlet is fitted by
making a small hole in the
vacuum bag and passing the
body of the outlet through from
the inside. Next to the vacuum
bag on the outside is a gasket
(shown by the dark line) on top
of which is a metal load
spreading ring. The assembly is
clamped up using a threaded
ring, in this case a knurled
version for hand tightening.

B A simple threaded tube
clamped by nuts to a rigid area
of the mould. These are usually
placed off the component, that
is on a flange, or on an area of
the component that will be cut
away during finishing.

C This outlet is fitted in the
same manner as B, but has a
shut-off valve.

D A vacuum outlet fitted under
the edge of the vacuum bag. It
can be formed from metal tubing
or the vacuum pipe itself. The
method is to wrap a piece of
vacuum sealing tape around the
pipe, stick it to the tape running
around the flange, then let the
vacuum-bag material form
around the pipe rather like
creating a tuck. The advantage
of using a short length of metal
tubing is that the whole
assembly can be laid up, then
taken to the pump and the
vacuum pipe simply pushed on.

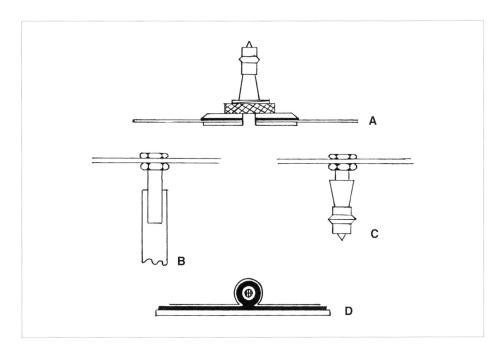

on to its end. The advantages of doing this are that the narrow metal pipe
will be less difficult to seal into the bag, while the vacuum pipe can be connected or disconnected with ease.

Curing under vacuum

Before turning on the vacuum pump, the bag should be tucked into all the
corners of the mould, spreading the slack material around it. There must
be enough slack in the bag that it can reach all the corners and detail of
the mould without being put under tension. At this stage, the vacuum
pump can be turned on. The time taken for the pump to pull all the air out
of the bag will vary. The larger the mould, or slacker the bag, the longer it
will take. The size of the pump and vacuum pipe will also affect the evac-
uation time. However, as long as the resin in the lamination has not started to go off, or cure, the time taken to extract the air is not critical.

The bag will begin to move soon after the pump has been turned on.
Wait until it begins to take the shape of the mould, then make any final
adjustments to its position, making sure that it is tucked into any tight corners. It is essential that the bag is not allowed to stretch across any corners or other detail. Also, the tucks or folds in the bag can be made to form
where best suited. For example, where a horizontal part of the mould
changes to a vertical face, it is a good idea to form a fold along that edge,
although it may not always be possible to do this exactly. When the bag
begins to stick to the mould, any areas where the bag is not in contact with
the mould wall will become more obvious. If a vacuum is being pulled and
the bag is becoming too difficult to move, turn off the pump. It may be necessary to break the seal of the bag and let in a little air to reduce the vacuum until you are able to adjust the bag as required. When you are happy,
the vacuum pump can be turned on and left running. At this point, the vacuum bag will look quite strange and untidy, with its many folds and creases, but this is normal and is not a cause for concern.

You can test whether a good vacuum has been achieved by pulling on
one of the folds in the bag: you should be unable to lift the bag away from
the mould's surface. Another widely used method of checking the vacuum

is to put a vacuum gauge in the bag. This can be done by fitting the bag with a two-piece take-off, similar to a vacuum take-off, or by putting a short length of pipe into the edge of the bag via the sealing strip. The advantage of the two-piece adaptor is that it will incorporate a non-return valve, which will allow the gauge to be connected to check the vacuum and then removed without loss of vacuum. This means that one gauge could be used to check several moulds at the same time.

When you appear to have obtained a good vacuum, check the bag for leaks. To do this, simply listen: bad leaks will produce a very noticeable hiss, but you will need to put an ear closer to find smaller leaks. Most leaks will occur where the bag is stuck to the sealing tape and, when located, can be cured by thumb pressure in the area of the leak. If, however, you discover a leak in the vacuum bag material itself, simply take a piece of sealing tape, leave the backing paper in place, and press it over the leak.

With any leaks rectified, a good vacuum should be easy to achieve and maintain. If a gauge is used, at least 0.7 bar (20in of mercury) should be shown as a minimum; 0.8 bar (25in or more of mercury) is excellent.

The mould can now be left to allow the cure to take place, and vacuum should be maintained until a fairly advanced stage of cure has been reached; with epoxy resins, this can take several hours. In some cases, when slow hardeners are being used, the pump may have to be left running for up to ten hours for the laminate to cure. As a means of checking the state of cure, when laminating, take some small offcuts of the glass fabric used in the laminated component, wet them out on a piece of polythene, then laminate together the same number of plies as there are in the laminate. Lay this small sample laminate on top of the mould so that it is in the same atmospheric conditions. This test piece can be checked from time to time; when it has hardened, turn off the vacuum pump, but leave the mould untouched until the laminate is fully cured. As previously mentioned, the cure time will depend on the resin type and make, the speed of the hardener and the conditions at the time of lamination. The manufacturer's data should give a good indication of the cure times for a particular resin and hardener.

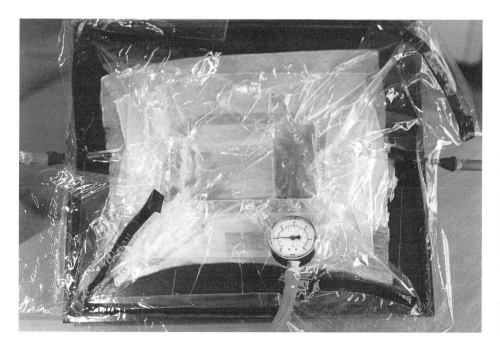

An epoxy lamination under vacuum for the cure. Although there are many creases and folds in the vacuum bag, note that it is held tightly against the inner face of the mould. This demonstrates the level of vacuum and, if the pump is turned off, will indicate the presence of any leaks.

An important point to remember is that unless the pump is fitted with a non-return valve, it should be disconnected when switched off. Otherwise, the vacuum in the bag may pull the oil out of the pump and into the bag.

The method of making a vacuum bag described here is considered a one-off job, the bag being disposable. In some cases, however, this type of vacuum bag can be carefully unsealed and used again.

Rubber vacuum bags

There are other methods of making vacuum bags, the most popular being the use of rubber, often silicone rubber. When the component is flat or of very shallow shape, rubber sheeting can be utilized. This can be purchased in various thicknesses, and the flatter the component, the thicker the sheet that can be used. Components with more pronounced shapes need a thinner rubber sheet, but if the shape is too complex to use a sheet, the vacuum bag must be made with liquid rubber. Again, silicone rubber is the most common, although sometimes latex is used.

In most cases, liquid rubbers are two-part compounds, and the mixing ratios and other technical details will vary from make to make. Consequently, you should always consult the manufacturer's data sheet.

When making a vacuum bag with liquid rubber, the basic technique is to coat the mould with a layer of the rubber mix, allow it to cure, then simply peel off the resultant rubber bag, which will be a perfectly tailored fit in the mould. If the mould is of a relatively simple shape, with no deep channels or sharp detail, the rubber can be sprayed or brushed directly on to its surface. It is a self-releasing material, so there is no need for a release agent. If there are deep channels or other detail, a layer of suitable material, similar in thickness to the proposed laminate, should be put in the mould prior to the application of the rubber. One method of doing this is to use pattern makers' sheet wax, which is obtainable in a variety of thicknesses. This can be formed in the mould by hand, using a warm air blower of some kind to soften the wax, or some other means of warming the sheet. Alternatively, the mould itself can be warmed. Carefully shape the wax into the mould to represent the laminated component, then apply the rubber over the wax. When the rubber has cured, peel it from the mould and remove the wax. Some laminators make a tailored rubber vacuum bag by laminating a cheap polyester component in the mould, then use it as a basis on which to form the rubber.

Tailored rubber vacuum bags have several advantages. Their fit and elasticity ensure a good even pressure on the lamination, whatever the shape, while they have a long life and can be used many times. Because they are shaped, they are quick to fit and put under vacuum, and no sealing tape is required, except where the shape of the mould's edge is complex. The normal method of sealing a rubber bag is with a metal frame that matches the shape of the flange around the mould. When the vacuum bag is in place, the frame is laid on top of the rubber resting on the flange. Then it is clamped down so that the rubber forms its own seal. If the mould flange is so complex in shape that making a metal frame would be difficult, a satisfactory alternative can be made by laminating a GRP version. When making a GRP frame, ensure that it is at least 4-5mm (⅙-⅕in) thick, so that it is stiff enough to transmit the pressure applied by the clamps. Some commercially-made vacuum bags have a metal frame bonded into the edge, while the associated mould can have over-centre clamps bolted permanently in position. This type of bag and clamping arrangement are normally chosen for long-term use, or where large numbers of components are planned, justifying the extra expense.

Finishing the component

When the lamination has cured completely, the vacuum bag can be removed, taking extra care if it is to be used again. The air bleed layer and the release layer should be removed. In some epoxy laminations, there may also be a peel ply. This is a woven nylon-type material, which is laid directly on to the lamination after the last ply has been put in place. When peeled from the cured surface, it leaves a finely textured finish. This is a result of the excess resin being forced into the weave and pulled off with the nylon material. The purpose can be to remove excess resin, or to produce a surface that is suitable for painting or for bonding on another component at a later stage. When painting or secondary bonding is to be carried out, the peel ply can be left in place until the component has been trimmed and finished. This will protect the surface until needed.

An epoxy component can be removed from its mould in the same manner as a polyester item; the trimming and finishing techniques are also the same. However, an epoxy part will be noticeably tougher, which does not make trimming any more difficult, but does produce nice clean edges. Moreover, due to the better stability offered by epoxy laminations, where the finished component consists of more than one part bonded together at a second stage, the parts should maintain a better fit because there will be less distortion during the cure. The extra stability also means that where parts are intended to fit up to others, but not be bonded together (for example, a hatch cover, a cowling, a door, etc), the fit will remain good with the passing of time.

Epoxy components take most types of paint very well, which means that a very good finish can be achieved and will last. The advantages of a finished epoxy component can be very desirable but the manufacture is more complicated, and the material costs are much higher.

No description of an epoxy process method can be complete, as there are endless variations of material, while the best method of making any particular component must be given careful thought. For example, the text describes making a vacuum bag on a simple rectangular mould and, although the principle is the same, a round or complex-shaped mould would need extra thought, but only in respect of the number of tucks or folds needed, and where to put them. Once the basic principle of manufacture is understood, adapting it to any particular application will be a matter of common sense and, obviously, practice. Furthermore, with experience, most laminators develop their own variations and methods.

Although this book is primarily about laminating with glass fibres, when epoxy resins are being used, a wider range of reinforcements can be employed, although the laminating technique remains the same. Carbon fibre fabrics or unidirectional fibres can help maximize stiffness in a lightweight component, while Kevlar fabrics can be used to achieve the lightest possible component with this method of lamination. More information on these and other fabrics can be obtained from your materials supplier.

The method for making a moulded rubber vacuum bag. The mould is shown containing a former to represent the intended component. Normally, this would be made from GRP or pattern makers' sheet wax of similar thickness to the component. It is coated with a two-part rubber mix to the required thickness: the more complex the component shape, the thinner the rubber bag. The supplier's data sheet will help on this point. The most commonly used materials are silicone rubber, latex and polyurethane; there are many versions of each type. In most cases, the resultant vacuum bag can be used without sealing tape. Instead, a pressure bar or frame, as shown in the diagram, and clamps will be sufficient.

7

Phenolic laminating

Phenolic resins have extremely good fire-retardant properties, and also good surface-spread-of-flame resistance. As a result, whenever phenolics are utilized, it is invariably to take advantage of these properties. In addition to excellent fire resistance, phenolics give off fewer toxic fumes and less smoke than most other resins when enough heat is produced to make them burn. Phenolic resins are employed in a variety of materials, among them rigid foam (used in sandwich panels) and solid tooling block (from which patterns are machined). Some forms of adhesive are also based on phenolic resins, but the resins discussed here are those formulated for wet laminating, with their special qualities enhanced.

Although phenolic resins do produce quite sturdy laminates, they are not used primarily in structural applications, except where their fire-retardant properties are essential: for example, in ship or boat interiors. Aircraft interiors are made with phenolic resins, but by a totally different method, while rail vehicles utilize laminated phenolics. In both cases, the structural performance will be important, but fire resistance is the main reason for their use.

In the main, phenolics are used with woven glass reinforcements, and are laminated into moulds made in exactly the same way as for polyester and epoxy laminating. Liquid release agents tend to be favoured when laminating phenolics and, as already mentioned, these can be bought in aerosol form or in tins for application by brush.

A few companies have attempted to produce phenolic gel coat materials, but they are difficult to manufacture and rarely available. However, polyester gel coats work satisfactorily with phenolic laminates, although their use does impair the fire-retardant properties. Providing a partial solution to this problem are low-viscosity gel coats with a different chemical formulation that produce a very thin final coat. Although their fire-retardant properties are not as good as phenolics, they are better than polyesters and, being very thin, these gel coats only cause a marginal reduction in fire resistance or surface spread of flame. It is advisable to consult your supplier to establish what materials are available at the time and whether they are suitable for the proposed project. One of the most widely used methods of overcoming the lack of phenolic gel coats is to laminate without a gel coat, then apply a fire-retardant paint to the completed component. In many cases, however, the laminate may be made in phenolic because of its low toxicity levels when burnt, and the surface finish may not be the prime consideration.

A section of pipe laminated with phenolic resin and woven glass. Its purpose was to act as ducting for boats and ships, phenolic materials being chosen for their excellent fire and smoke properties.

The reason it is difficult to produce reliable phenolic gel coats is because phenolic resins produce water during the cure. With the gel coat being applied to the mould surface, the water cannot escape and tends to upset the surface finish. Gel coats aside, this problem can make it difficult to obtain a good surface finish any way, although the problem will be less noticeable with a thin laminate, as most or all of the water will be able to escape through the back of the laminate. Phenolics also change colour during the cure, and this continues after the laminate is fully cured. Light has a marked effect on the colour of unpainted phenolic laminates, which is why it is not practical to attempt to add colour to phenolic gel coats.

Two-part systems
Most phenolic laminating resin systems are two-part compounds, and the relevant data sheet should be consulted for the correct mixing ratio. Most suppliers will offer hardeners with different activity levels, and obtaining

the most suitable version for the proposed project is very important. The percentage of hardener to resin is usually slightly higher than with polyesters, but like polyesters, the amount of hardener affects the pot life. With phenolics, the cure begins immediately the mix is made. Therefore, it is important to have the right hardener for the job in hand and be aware of the correct mixing ratio.

It is essential not to try to extend the pot life by using less than the recommended amount of hardener, otherwise the laminate will remain in a soft uncured state for a very long time. There is also the danger of the laminate never reaching a fully cured state. If the recommended level of hardener is exceeded, you may find the resin becoming too viscose to laminate before the job is complete.

Processing techniques

Phenolics vary considerably from one manufacturer to another in the way they are processed, that is mixing ratio and the type of hardener. However, they are laminated in almost the same manner as epoxy systems. Since the reinforcement is likely to be a woven fabric or stitched unidirectional material, the relevant shapes can be cut with the aid of templates, as described in Chapter 6.

With the mould prepared, brush a generous coat of the mixed resin over the surface, then place the first piece of fabric into the mould. This should be wetted out by brushing just enough resin into the fabric to saturate it, although an excess of resin should be avoided. When the first ply has been wetted out, repeat the process for the second ply, and so on until the required number of plies is in place.

In most cases, this type of laminate should be cured under vacuum, which is carried out in the same manner as for an epoxy laminate. When the mould or laminate is of a shallow or very simple shape, it is possible to allow the cure to take place without vacuum pressure. However, since woven glass will not remain in tight corners or sharp detail while in the wet state, the decision to cure without pressure should be taken carefully.

When the component is large or complex, it is important to select a hardener that will give sufficient pot life to allow completion of the laminate and enough time to put it under vacuum. If, however, the shape is simple, and vacuum will not be used, the lamination can be carried out with several mixes, provided the laminate made with each mix is fully consolidated before the mix goes off. Normally, the wetted out fabric will be consolidated with a brush; rollers are not often used with phenolic or epoxy laminates, but if you find that a roller helps, there is no reason why it should not be used. In fact, all laminating techniques, regardless of the resin type, are open to individual interpretation, once you know what the end result should be and understand the basic method of achieving it.

Post cure

Phenolic components are often given a post cure, which helps to achieve the maximum performance from the laminate, i.e. its fire-retardant or any other special properties. Post cures are usually carried out in a large oven, or an insulated box or room, the temperatures and times varying with each manufacturer's formulation. The data sheet for the material being used will provide this information. As a guide, a typical post cure would take place at a temperature of 45-60°C (113-140°F) for 8-12 hours. With very large components, the lower end of the temperature range should be used for an extended period. Although post cures are widely employed when laminating with phenolic resin, they are not imperative. If a post cure is not carried out, the laminated component will still achieve most, if not all, of its potential performance, but this process will take longer, and there is no certain way of determining when the maximum cure and performance have been achieved. This simply means that the finished component should be left for as long as practical before putting it into service if maximum performance is a requirement of the laminate.

A post cure should be carried out after removing the component from the mould, but before any trimming and finishing. This is because the task will be kinder to sanding discs when the resin is harder. Components can be removed from their moulds in exactly the same manner as polyester and epoxy components.

Surface finish
One point to note about phenolic laminates is their surface finish which, sometimes, may be marred by pin-holes. The scale of this condition will not be constant: some components will be worse than others, or the problem may not occur at all. The colour will also vary considerably from one component to another, some looking very blotchy. Post curing may make the uneven colour look worse, while the colour will change when exposed to light. None of these conditions affects the performance of the laminate. It must be remembered that phenolics behave in this way, and some of the processing difficulties must be tolerated if the special qualities of phenolics are to be enjoyed.

8

Positive-pressure laminating with matched moulds

The method of curing laminated components under vacuum is widely used, but there is another method of curing under pressure, known as positive pressure. For this, a second mould is required to form the reverse face of the component. In effect, this is matched-mould laminating. However, the technique is not suitable for all applications: it may not be practical to use this method with moulds that are particularly large or of a very complex shape.

To produce the back mould, some form of pattern will be required. If possible, when creating the pattern for the main mould, make it a direct copy of the component to be moulded, including the wall thickness. After attaching weirs to form the edge flanges, you can take a mould off the face of the pattern, as described in Chapter 4. Then the weirs should be removed and a mould taken off the back. When the pattern has been removed, the result will be a pair of moulds with a space between that represents the exact form of the intended component.

If making an exact replica of the component as a pattern is not possible, there is another excellent method of achieving the same result. A normal pattern should be made to duplicate the face side of the component, and a mould complete with edge flanges made from it. Next, a suitable material should be put into the mould to represent the laminated component, including the correct wall thickness. Finally, a second mould can be taken off the back of this material.

There are two main methods of representing the laminated component in the master mould. One is actually to laminate a dummy component in the mould. This should be trimmed as appropriate and the reverse face smoothed, either by sanding the laminate, or by covering it with a layer of body filler and sanding this smooth when set. A suitable release procedure should be carried out and, with this mocked-up component back in the mould, a second mould can be taken off the back. Another excellent technique is to use pattern makers' sheet wax. A thickness that matches the intended component's wall thickness should be chosen; with gentle warming, it will form readily to the contours of the mould. This material can also be easily trimmed to represent the component. Because it is wax, no release is required. As before, a second mould can be taken off.

With both moulds having been given a suitable release treatment, the laminating process can be carried out in the master mould, using normal techniques. The important point is to ensure that the lamination has a wall

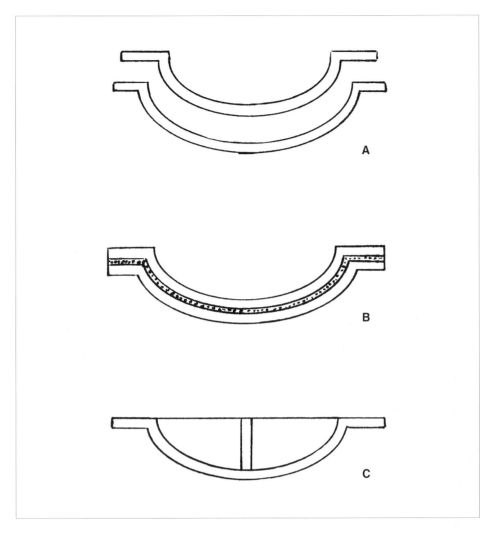

thickness of not less than the space between the two moulds. Ideally, the wet lamination should be very slightly thicker than this cavity.

With the component laminated, the back mould should be put into place and pressure applied by some form of clamp to close the two parts of the mould together. It is difficult to measure the pressure applied in this way, but this is of no great importance; even pressure over the entire mould area is far more critical. An aid to achieving even pressure is to make the back mould as thick as practical, which will help distribute the force. If, as suggested, the wet laminate is marginally thicker than the cavity, a good even pressure will result. Another often used method of applying pressure to matched moulds is to put the assembly in a vacuum bag. This will apply even pressure automatically; the vacuum should be maintained until the resin has cured.

Some may question the idea of making matched moulds, then using vacuum pressure for the cure. However, apart from ensuring a perfectly consolidated void-free laminate, matched moulds will produce a component with a very constant wall thickness and an excellent smooth finish on the reverse face. For certain components, and when several identical items must be made, the extra cost and effort needed to make matched tooling is well worth it. With polyesters, mechanical clamping of this type is essential; curing these under vacuum is not recommended, as the vacuum will pull the styrenes out of the resin, preventing it from reaching its fully cured stage.

9

Spray laminating

Another method of utilizing polyester resin and chopped glass fibres is to spray laminate them. The resultant laminates will be similar in performance, and can be utilized in similar applications, to components made by hand lay-up techniques. The basic principle is to spray catalysed resin at the same time as the chopped glass fibres into the mould. The laminate is consolidated with a roller, in similar fashion to a normal wet lay-up. Spray laminating is ideal for certain applications, but is not suitable for small moulds or moulds of complex shape. It works well on large areas and comparatively simple shapes.

Normally, two types of equipment are available for this, one being a twin-pot machine, in other words, a spray gun with twin nozzles. One nozzle delivers accelerated resin, while the other sprays catalysed resin. The separation of the resin in this way prevents any stage of cure taking place in the gun; the resin is pumped directly from the drum in which it is contained. The other equipment uses a gun with a single nozzle, catalyst being metered into the accelerated resin as it passes through the nozzle. Both systems spray resin on to the mould surface, while a glass roving chopper ejects the fibres at the same time. The chopped fibres usually measure 20-40mm (¾-1½in) long.

As can be seen, expensive equipment is needed for the process, but the cost can be offset by the savings made when longer runs of components are planned.

Since spray laminating does not employ glass matt of a given weight, the reinforcement can't be used to gauge the thickness of the finished laminate. However, it is estimated that one pass of the spray gun will result in a thickness of 1-1.5mm (½₅-¹⁄₁₆in) after it has been rolled.

Mould preparation and release are carried out in the same way as for normal hand lay-up with polyester resin. Then resin and chopped glass fibres are sprayed into the mould in as even a coating as possible, rather like spraying paint. After every second pass or coat, the wet laminate should be consolidated with a laminating roller. The thickness of the laminate must not exceed 6-7mm (¼-⁵⁄₁₆in) at any one time, otherwise distortion of the component may occur. This could result from an exotherm, caused by the faster catalyst normally employed in this type of laminating. If, for some reason, the component has to be much thicker, the first 6-7mm (¼-⁵⁄₁₆in) of the laminate should be allowed to cure, after which further material can be sprayed on. However, this is not likely to occur very often, as most GRP applications requiring wall thicknesses of greater than 7mm

(⁵⁄₁₆in) will be of a more structural nature (large boat or ship hulls, for instance) and, therefore, would utilize woven reinforcement. Once the resin and glass have been sprayed into the mould, the component can be completed in exactly the same manner as a hand laminated part.

Pros and cons

As with any manufacturing system, there are advantages and disadvantages to spray laminating. One of the advantages is that it takes far less time to spray a given area than to laminate it by hand. This also means that you can employ a faster catalyst. These two points add up to faster mould turn-round. The technique is claimed to be less wasteful on materials, although there is considerable overspray when covering the outer edges of the mould. The degree of overspray will depend on the shape of the mould. Some laminators overcome this problem by hand laminating a band of chopped strand matt around the outer edge of the mould. Then the layer of sprayed resin and glass does not have to be taken so close to the edge. There is no weighing or mixing, which reduces waste, as you only use the amount of resin and glass needed to cover the mould. Spraying is less labour intensive, while the glass rovings used in the chopper are cheaper, weight for weight, than chopped strand matt.

A disadvantage is the capital outlay and, despite claims to the contrary, it can be a messy operation. The equipment needs thorough and frequent maintenance, and a fair degree of skill is needed to obtain an even thickness. Moreover, the process is only suitable for certain applications.

The resin used for spray laminating is usually of low viscosity to ensure fast wetting out of the glass, but where the mould has vertical or steeply angled sides, it needs to be thixotropic to prevent it from running.

Spray application of glass fibres and polyester resin has a great deal to offer in some applications, but it is unlikely to be practical for small components or one-off projects, or for those who have little or no experience of GRP processes. However, if the process seems particularly suitable for a potential project, like any other, the technique can be learned by anyone with the determination to succeed.

Although spray laminating equipment will vary from one manufacturer to another, the basic operating principle remains the same.

93

10

Closed-mould laminating (RTM)

Matched moulds, like those described in Chapter 9, are used as a means of processing glass-fibre matt and polyester resin in a technique known as resin-transfer moulding (RTM). The two-part moulds are made in GRP, in a similar fashion to those described previously, but there are some important differences. Firstly, they must be far more substantial with a greater wall thickness. Also, the flanges around both sections of the mould must be robust enough to accommodate a seal, which will effectively close the mould when the two halves are put together.

The mould seal may be made in a variety of ways. For example, a trough can be formed in the edge flange of one half of the mould when it is made. Then a silicone rubber section can be fixed in the trough so that it stands proud of the flange surface to seal against the face of the adjoining mould flange. Alternatively, a rubber section can be simply bonded to the face of one flange. Both methods employ ready-made silicone or other rubber sections. However, a seal can be made by the laminator, using two-part silicone rubber mix, although some form of mould would be required for casting the liquid rubber to the required shape. Flange gaskets or seals can also be cut from suitable rubber sheeting.

The face of each section of the mould should be release treated in the same manner as for hand lay-up. If necessary, a gel coat can be applied, but in many cases, components formed by this process do without. When a self-coloured component is required, the resin being used for the lamination can be pigmented as required. If the mould has a good surface, the component will have a nice finish, although the glass matt may be close to the surface. However, if no further surface finishing is being carried out, this should not be a problem.

Resin flow

With the two halves of the mould prepared, the glass matt is placed dry into the female portion, and the mould closed. Although chopped strand matt can be used for some RTM applications, special glass matts are available that ensure improved resin flow. These matts can also be preformed by pressing them in a cheap mould made for the purpose, heat being used to set the matt into shape. Preforming not only speeds the process, but also makes it cleaner and neater.

Resin is injected into the mould through an inlet, which is usually placed near the centre of the component, while vents at the most distant points from the inlet allow air to escape in front of the advancing resin.

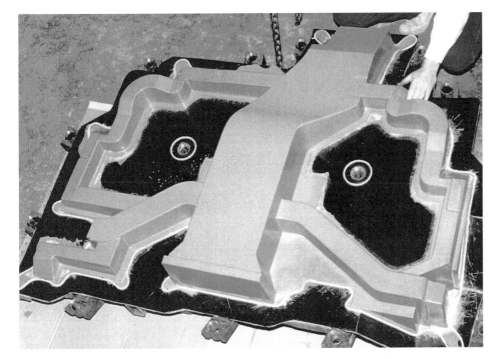

Left and below left **These photographs show an excellent example of RTM. At the top is one half of the mould after separation; below, the component after removal from the mould. Note the minimal amount of finishing required of a component of this complexity.**

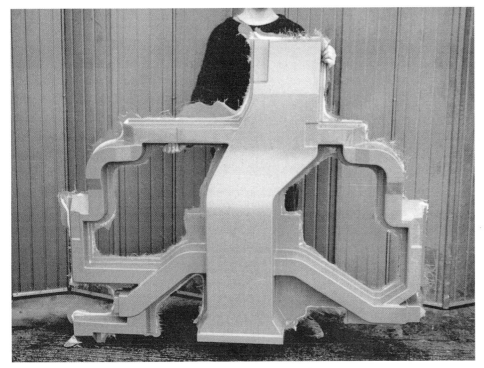

When all the air has escaped and neat resin is beginning to flow from the vents, the supply pipe is clamped off. At this point, the mould is allowed to stand until the cure is complete.

The RTM process can be carried out with varying degrees of sophistication and, in many cases, users devise their own variations of the basic technique, often as simple as possible to minimize cost. The resin can be mixed by hand and supplied under pressure from a simple pressure pot, which is readily available. This is connected to the mould inlet by a pipe with a tap that controls the flow of resin. A length of clear plastic pipe connected to the air vent side of the mould indicates when all the air has been forced out by the resin. Alternatively, the same type of mould can be employed, but the resin is held in a drum without catalyst, being pumped

Right and below right **Two views of a vehicle roof manufactured by the RTM method.**

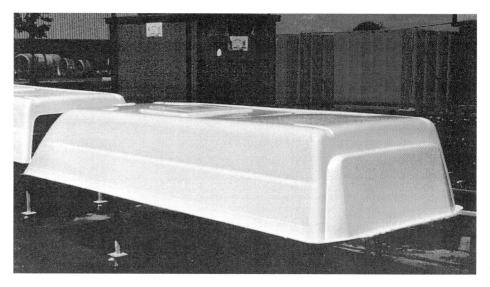

through a special lance, where the correct amount of catalyst is added as it passes through the nozzle. When the mould is ready for the resin, the lance is simply pushed into the inlet and resin pumped into the mould. Many factories use the resin-transfer moulding process, but employ automatic or semi-automatic systems, where the moulds are opened and closed hydraulically and the uncatalysed resin pumped through a metering nozzle. In some cases, the correct amount of resin is delivered automatically, then the machine cuts off and carries out a cleaning routine in preparation for the next cycle. These advanced types of automatic moulding machine can also have a built-in mould pressure control. Apart from laying the preformed glass fibre in the mould and removing the finished component, the entire process is automatic.

Process time

Components made by the RTM process are normally excellent in appearance and have as good a surface finish on the reverse face as on the front, which can be important when the component is to be some form of cover or case, or an enclosure of some kind. It also ensures that the component has an even and constant wall thickness. The process is suitable for use when large numbers of components are planned on a production-line basis, the very quick process time helping to make it a viable option, even with a simple completely manual set-up. Process time can be as little as eight or ten minutes, while the turn-round time on a fully automatic system can be as little as five minutes. The latter is due, in part, to the extremely short automatic cleaning process.

However, RTM is an expensive process from the beginning. The pattern must be double-sided, and the two-part mould much more substantial. In most cases, the mould will need an external framework, usually of steel, to prevent it from being distorted by injection pressure. The seal around the mould adds to the cost, especially if the mould is custom made, while the cost of the special resin injection equipment increases with the level of sophistication.

The process can produce good results with the simple pressure pot, rubber feed pipe and very basic mould seals, but at this level, skill and experience are needed to achieve consistency. When working with such basic equipment, important considerations are the resin type and a catalyst to suit the estimated process time, that is the time it takes to fill the mould and for the resin to cure. The pressure requirement for the feed pot is also crucial. Normally, this is comparatively low, but it should be checked with the material supplier, as the viscosity of the resin will vary from one manufacturer to another, which will have an effect on the pressure requirement. With more sophisticated equipment, the pressure is controlled automatically.

When considering resin-transfer moulding, it is advisable to consult a GRP supplier prior to starting. Outline the proposed project and ask for recommendations for the most suitable materials for the finished component and the level of equipment needed to carry out the process.

Vacuum transfer

There are simpler variations of RTM that don't utilize positive pressure to inject the resin. One of these still requires matched two-part moulds,

The roof mould being sprayed
with a gel coat.

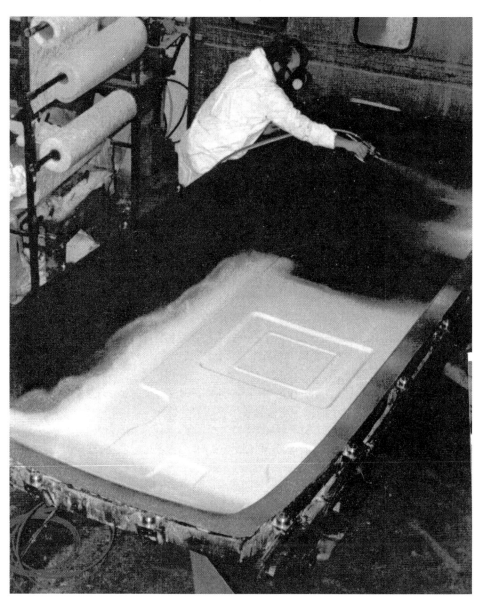

The dry carrier being put in
place prior to closing the mould.

which are prepared as described previously, but the resin is transferred to the mould by a combination of gravity and vacuum. A reservoir holding sufficient resin to fill the mould cavity is held above the level of the mould and attached to the feed pipe supplying the cavity. A vent or vents on the opposite side of the mould are connected to a vacuum pump. As the resin enters the mould by gravity, the air is drawn off by the pump. Lengths of clear plastic pipe (reinforced fuel pipe is ideal) incorporated in the outlets will show when all the air has been extracted and the mould is full of resin. Then the pipes can be clamped and the component left to cure.

This method can work very well, but care must be taken to position the outlet or outlets correctly. If the component is of a complex shape and only one outlet is used, it is possible for the incoming resin to flow past a section and leave a pocket of trapped air. Once the resin begins to flow from the outlet and the vacuum pipe is clamped off, any air still in the mould will remain there. This is why, in some cases, it is necessary to incorporate more than one outlet. The outlet pipe must be clamped off before the resin can reach the vacuum pump, otherwise it will cause irreparable damage.

The advantage of using clear plastic pipe at the outlets, and simply clamping it to stop the resin flow, is that no cleaning is required. When the resin in the mould has cured, you simply cut off the length of pipe containing cured resin and throw it away. It just means the loss of a short piece of cheap plastic pipe with every component.

Correct positioning of the inlet and outlet, or outlets, is essential. When more than one outlet is employed, T-pieces should be used to join the pipes so that all the outlets are connected to one vacuum pump. Since the resin relies on gravity to flow into the mould, the inlet should be placed at the highest point, while the outlets should be at the extremities. Obviously, the shape of the component will dictate the exact positioning of the inlet and outlets, and also the number of the latter.

As with normal RTM, the special glass matt can be preformed; if the component is of a comparatively simple shape, standard chopped strand

The closed mould. Note the substantial framework required to resist the internal pressure generated by the RTM process.

matt can also be employed. It is advisable to use a resin at the lower end of the viscosity range for vacuum transfer. Also, since the process is slower than when injecting resin under pressure, the catalyst should not be too fast. The resin supplier will be able to suggest the best catalyst and specify the mixing ratio for the resin supplied.

This method of resin transfer can work very well, but the slower catalyst means that the cure will take longer, so the whole cycle requires more time than when injecting resin under pressure. Moreover, there is always a slight chance of an occasional bubble due to trapped air.

Using a vacuum bag

Another variation of RTM also utilizes vacuum to ensure resin transfer, but only a single-sided mould is required. The glass matt is cut to shape, or preformed, and laid in the mould. Then a vacuum bag is formed over the open side, exactly as described for curing epoxy laminations in Chapter 6. When using this method, it is advisable to place the vacuum bag sealing tape as close to the edge of the actual mould as possible. This helps to contain the resin. An inlet should be put in under the edge of the vacuum bag, together with an outlet or outlets. As in the previous method, resin is gravity fed to the mould and vacuum applied to the outlet side. The vacuum assists the transfer of the resin, and it also applies pressure to the glass matt as it is resinated, in the same manner as when laminating with epoxy resin.

Although the vacuum bag method of resin transfer will produce components of satisfactory mechanical performance, their appearance will not be as good as that of components from matched moulds. The face side, that is the surface adjacent to the mould face, would be comparable with a matched-mould component, but the reverse face would have a finish that showed it had been formed by a flexible vacuum bag. The exceptions to this situation are components of simple enough shape that they can be formed with the aid of a caul plate. This is a type of diaphragm, made from

An automated set-up for the RTM process.

A conical moulding made by the RTM method. In this particular case, a lightweight foam core has been utilized.

material with a degree of flexibility, but which is stiff enough to distribute the pressure of the vacuum bag over the resinated glass matt. The use of a caul plate would improve the finish of the reverse face of the component. Basically, a caul plate acts like a thin floating matched mould, and it should be placed on the glass matt before the vacuum bag is formed over the mould. It is essential to put a release film between the glass matt and the caul plate, otherwise the latter will become part of the component.

Caul plates can be made from a variety of materials: heat-formable plastic sheet is good, as is a thin GRP laminate. The latter would allow a caul plate with a more complex shape to be made. If the proposed component warrants the time and expense, a good method of producing a caul plate is first to laminate a dummy component in the mould by the normal hand lay-up technique, but to make this lay-up slightly thinner than the intended component. If different thicknesses of glass matt are available, use the same number of plies for the dummy component, but employ a thinner glass matt for one of the plies. If different thicknesses of matt are not to hand, leave one ply out of the lay-up. When cured, remove and trim the dummy component. Then cover the reverse face with filler, sand this down to a smooth finish and, when all the texture of the chopped strand matt has been smoothed out, apply a wax release agent. If available, use PVA as well. Return the dummy component to the mould, then laminate the caul plate with a thin lay-up: a single ply of something like 450g/sq.m (1½oz/sq.ft) matt would suffice. You could use a gel coat to obtain a good finish, but this is not essential.

Vacuum assisted resin transfer is claimed to be quicker than hand lay-up, but if a hand tailored vacuum bag is being used, there is some doubt about this. If, however, you use a moulded silicone rubber vacuum bag, the process time will be quicker. The resin must still be mixed by hand, but no brushes or rollers are used. This method could be quicker than hand lay-up, but to some degree, the component's size and configuration will decide its suitability.

11

Foam as a core material

When used in conjunction with laminated glass fibres, foam makes an excellent core material. It comes in a variety of types and has a wide range of applications: from forming stiffening stringers in boat hulls to acting as the core of the component itself, a surfboard for example.

In many cases, foam is employed to produce a light, yet stiff, component. One very common application is to use flat sheets of foam to make panels for truck bodies and the like. In most cases with this type of panel, the glass-fibre skins are pre-made and bonded to the foam core as a second operation. However, when the foam has a more complex shape, the glass-fibre skins are laminated directly on to the core, or laminated into a mould and the core formed with two-part liquid foam.

There are many types of foam, including some very expensive aircraft-quality versions that are resistant to high temperatures and to most resins, but these are less common. Polystyrene, polyurethane and PVC foams are normally used for GRP work; all are available through GRP suppliers.

Polystyrene is the cheapest foam. It can be purchased in block or sheet form and is easy to cut. The blocks and sheets can be joined together with PVA wood glue to achieve a required shape or thickness, then trimmed by sawing or sanding, or by the use of a hot-wire cutter. However, polystyrene foam is dissolved by polyester resin, so a barrier layer must be applied to the foam before laminating the GRP skins to it. A popular method of doing this is to brush on one or two coats of domestic water-based emulsion paint; plaster or car body filler can also be used.

Although much more expensive than polystyrene, the most widely used of the common foams is polyurethane. It is not attacked by polyester resin and, therefore, does not need a barrier layer. It can be sawn and sanded with ease.

PVC foam is the most expensive of the trio. It is not attacked by polyester resin, so a barrier layer is not required, and it can be cut and shaped with electric or hand tools. One major advantage of PVC foam is that it provides a much better structural performance than polystyrene or polyurethane, both in compression and tension. This also gives the finished component better knock and vibration resistance. A disadvantage of PVC foam is that it produces very toxic fumes when burned. This applies to a lesser degree to the other foams described.

Rigid foams made from phenolic are also available. They are not usually chosen for true structural applications, as they are lower in cellular strength than other foams. In the main, they are used for their excellent fire-retardant properties, coupled with low smoke emissions when burned. Phenolics are widely employed in personnel carrying vehicles of all types, where they offer greater safety in the event of fire.

Where the use of phenolics seems appropriate, it is advisable to consult the manufacturer or supplier, who will provide guidance on their suitability, suggest the best type for the intended application, and issue processing instructions. These instructions will also specify the adhesive to use. It is important to use the correct adhesive, both from a technical standpoint and to avoid compromising the fire and smoke properties.

The manner in which a component is constructed, using foam as the core, will vary, depending on its shape and the facilities available. When flat panels are required, the foam is normally purchased in sheet form at the required thickness. Ready-made GRP sheets are also available for the skins, although you can make your own by laminating on to a smooth, flat surface, remembering that good release is important over large areas.

Adhesives

The most widely used adhesive for this type of construction is polyurethane, some examples of which foam as they cure, making them ideal for bonding the rough surfaces involved. Other adhesives that can be used are two-part epoxy, PVA and polyester. Whichever type is selected, some form of pressure must be applied to the panel during the cure, and a flat surface will be required on which to press the panel. Where panels are being made as production items, the pressure will be applied in a purpose-made press, or by means of a vacuum bag, the latter being widely used, as all that is required is a large flat bench and a vacuum pump. Static weights can also be employed, but the pressure must be spread evenly across the panel. One method of doing this is with bags of sand, which enable the surface to be covered fairly evenly; to achieve a good pressure, the bags can be stacked on top of each other. In all cases of making flat panels, it is advisable to lay thick steel or aluminium sheets on top of the panel, as these will distribute the pressure more evenly.

When the selected adhesive is a moisture activated polyurethane type, more attention must be paid to the application of pressure, as this type of adhesive expands during the cure, generating an internal pressure. If

A prime example of the use of a rigid foam core with GRP skins. After the foam has been shaped, the GRP is laminated on to it. In most cases, no mould is involved, although some foam-cored GRP surf and sail boards are made using moulds.

insufficient or uneven pressure is applied to the outside of the panel, the finished thickness is likely to be very uneven, and some nasty bumps may appear in the surface.

In most cases, the adhesive should be applied to the bottom skin of the panel, the core put in place (with any frames or inserts needed in the panel), then adhesive applied to the top skin before this, too, is added. If the panel is to be cured in a press, it is a good idea to cover it completely with a sheet of cheap industrial polythene, which can be reused. The lay-up should be slid into the press, the pressure set and the assembly left to cure. The techniques for using vacuum pressure are exactly the same as described elsewhere in this book, while the employment of static weights is self explanatory.

Practical considerations

When foam is being used to stiffen a structure such as a flat-sided tank that requires a smooth internal finish, the component should be made on a male mould. In this case, the first laminated skin is laid up on the mould, its last ply of chopped-strand matt being made very resin rich, then the sheets of foam are laid on to the wet laminate. Enough pressure must be applied to hold the foam in close contact with the laminate, but this need not be excessive. When the first skin has cured, the outer skin can be laminated over the foam. Again, the first ply should be resin rich.

For compound shapes, aerofoils and surfboards for example, the foam should be shaped to the required profile first. This can be done by hand or machine sanding or, in some cases, with a hot-wire cutter. This purpose-made gadget incorporates a taut wire, heated by electric current, that slices through the foam like a cheese cutter. However, it is only suitable for producing single-curve shapes or profiling flat sheets. If PVC foam is to be hot-wire cut, take extra care, as toxic fumes may be given off.

With the foam shaped, the skin can be laminated directly on to the foam. In the case of surfboards and similar components, fine woven glass fabric is used for the laminated skin. When cured, the skin is sanded to a smooth finish and polished. In some cases, a final coat of clear resin may be applied to produce a gloss finish.

Sometimes, a shaped foam core will be used in a mould where the laminated skins are made first, then the mould closed around the foam

Below **Rigid foam is commonly used as a core for flat panels. In this case, the foam is phenolic, as are the woven glass skins. Phenolics are normally used for their excellent smoke and fire-resistant properties.**

Below right **Honeycomb core materials are also available and offer greater structural performance than foam, although they are more expensive. In this case, aluminium honeycomb has been faced with woven glass skins. Honeycomb made from aramid fibres is available, as is paper honeycomb. The last is the least expensive of the three types, but offers the poorest structural performance.**

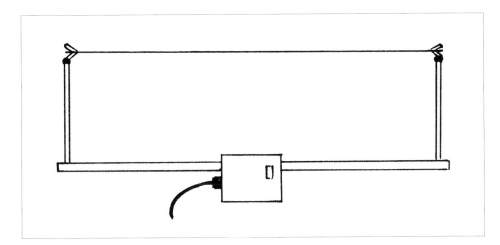

A hand-held version of a hot-wire cutter, which incorporates a transformer that reduces mains voltage to that required (usually 18 volts) to heat the nickel-chrome cutting wire. There are many versions of this simple tool, some being quite large and used in conjunction with a travelling bed for cutting big sheets and blocks.

with an adhesive between the core and skins. With this method, the foam must be shaped to a high degree of accuracy, while the pre-made laminated skins must be of constant thickness to ensure a match of skins and foam when put together. High spots will prevent the mould from closing, and low spots will result in voids. It is not easy to obtain a perfect match. The adhesive used to bond the foam to the skins will take care of some discrepancies, but this technique of utilizing foam as a core material is quite difficult to carry out successfully.

Another method of employing foam in compound shapes is to laminate the skins and allow them to cure, then close the mould and inject two-part liquid polyurethane foam through a hole provided in the mould for this purpose. As it cures, the foam will expand to fill the cavity. A small breather hole, at the other end of the mould, will allow air to escape as the foam expands, and act as an indicator that the mould is full.

The disadvantage of this method is that it offers no guarantee that it will fill the mould completely: the density of the cured foam can vary and it may contain air bubbles. These problems can be minimized by ensuring that sufficient foam is injected to fill the mould while it is still expanding. The data sheet for the foam will give the expansion ratio. With this information, all that is required is to calculate the volume of the cavity in the mould. You can then make sure that sufficient foam is mixed and injected.

The other major consideration with this method of using foam is that, due to the high internal pressure generated during the foaming process, the mould must be very substantial to resist distortion and being forced apart. Moulds made with this process in mind should be reinforced with longitudinal and transverse stiffeners. Alternatively, a steel framework can be built around the outside of the mould. When using liquid foam in a closed mould, it must be remembered that only the foam holds the skins together, since no adhesive can be introduced.

In GRP work, there will be many applications where foam offers advantages as a core material. The choice of foam type and the method by which it is used will depend on its cost, technical requirements, availability and the skill levels of the user. Often, a method of use will have to be devised by employing the basic principles outlined here. As with other GRP products, obtain a data sheet for the foam being used, as this will outline what can and cannot be done with it, as well as providing valuable technical information and safety advice.

Repairs & modifications

GRP components are used in a very wide range of applications, and some of these may require a long life. Any component that has a true working life (such as a car body, part of a machine, an item of sports equipment, etc) may suffer damage and, in some cases, the original mould may not exist any more, so a repair will become essential. There may also be occasions when an existing component does not quite meet the demands place upon it, but the cost of making a completely new replacement would be prohibitive, in which case the original item must be modified. The purpose of this chapter is to describe how those repairs and modifications can be carried out.

Basic repair techniques

When a laminated polyester component has been damaged and the laminate completely split (as might occur with a GRP car body involved in some sort of impact), the ideal treatment would be to put the component back into the mould, which would ensure perfect alignment of the damaged portion during the repair process. However, this is seldom possible, so we will assume that the repair is to be carried out without the use of the original mould.

When subjected to an impact of sufficient strength, a GRP component will typically display some compression damage, like a dent, where the laminate has failed around the compressed area, and there will be inevitable tears with the glass fibres protruding from the torn parts. To repair this type of damage, the main portions of the affected area must first be held as near to the original shape as possible. This will make some form of bracing necessary, and wood or metal will do. Since the repair work will begin on the reverse face of the laminate, the bracing must be put on the outside.

Any dent-like areas should be pushed out to resemble the original shape as closely as possible, while torn parts should be held in place by bracing. The fraying of the fibres around tears may make it difficult to fit the parts together. If this occurs, run a fine hand saw down each tear to remove the frayed fibres. This should make it easier to align the damaged parts. Rapid-set body filler is an excellent means of sticking the bracing in place. Using small blobs of filler and some battens, simply align the damaged parts and hold them in position. If any parts have broken off completely, but you still have them, hold them in place by the same method.

When the damaged area has been realigned as closely as possible, and held firmly by the bracing, any gaps or portions that are missing completely must be filled in. For small gaps and holes, modelling clay will do the job; for larger missing pieces, use card, aluminium or any other material that can be made to represent the missing piece. This type of infill does not have to duplicate the original shape exactly, but it should be as close to this as possible.

With everything aligned and firmly braced, the next stage is to sand the back of the laminate, working over the damaged portion and on to the undamaged surface around the area to be repaired. This not only provides a clean surface to which the repair can be bonded, but it also levels off the damaged area by removing any protruding pieces.

The next task is to laminate a patch over the damaged area, but there is a decision to be made at this point: should the patch be laminated with normal polyester resin or epoxy? Polyesters make excellent laminating resins and, if the laminate is polyester, they will effect a reasonable repair. However, polyesters are not the best adhesives, which may call the long-term adhesion of the repair into doubt. If the component leads a hard life and is likely to be damaged again or often, or the component is not intended for a long life, using polyester resin for the repair would be perfectly satisfactory. While repairs made with polyester could last a long time, if the component is important, valuable, rare or, for any other reason, needs the best repair possible, the patch should be laminated with epoxy resin, and the reinforcement should be woven glass fabric. Another good reason for using epoxy resin is that it produces a stronger repair.

The lamination on the reverse of the damage is the main strength of the repair, and the number of plies necessary for the patch will depend on the type of fabric used. Although almost any type of woven fabric will do, it is best not to use a very fine weave. Three or four plies should be strong enough for most repairs.

When the lamination on the back of the repair has cured fully, the bracing can be removed from the front of the component. The next stage is to take an electric sander and use the edge of the disc to cut along the torn parts, through to the newly laminated patch on the back. Take care, however, not to cut through the patch. Then open up the cuts to a wide V-shape, as wide as practical. Finally, use the face of the sanding disc to sand the entire damaged area, removing any paint and gel coat. If there are holes where pieces are missing, taper their edges at as flat an angle as possible. Again, take care not to cut into the repair patch.

Now the damaged face of the component can be repaired and, as before, you must choose between polyester and epoxy resin. While epoxy is stronger than polyester, the patch on the reverse face of the component provides the main strength of the repair, so the decision is not quite so critical. Again, woven fabric should be used, but not a heavy weave. The aim is to laminate strips of fabric into the wide V-shaped cuts and any areas where pieces of the original laminate are missing. Put in as many plies as practical, increasing the width of the strips as the cuts fill up, but there is no need to attempt to fill these areas completely. The laminated strips should be left to cure, after which the sander can be lightly run over the surface to remove any protruding bits of laminate. If the repair is being carried out on a very thick component (6mm/¼in or more), it will be possible to sand enough of the front face away to laminate a single ply over the entire area of the repair. However, for most normal thicknesses of laminate, there will not be enough material to do this.

The next stage is to level off the repair with commercial body filler. If there are any areas where this is likely to be very thick, it is best to build up the thickness in two or more applications. This will prevent too much heat from occurring during the cure, which can cause shrinkage and cracking when the filler has been sanded down to the original contours of the component.

At this point, the repair may be primed and painted, but it could be taken a stage further before painting. By sanding down the repair area a little more, a gel coat can be applied, which can be rubbed down and painted over. If the component was painted originally, this means that the new paint will sit on the same type of base and should weather in the same manner as the original. If the component has a self-coloured gel coat and no paint finish, it is possible to colour the gel coat of the repair, which can be rubbed down and polished. However, this is more difficult than it sounds, particularly if the area is quite large. A thick gel coat will be required, and the best method of achieving this is with two, or even three, coats, allowing each to cure partially before applying the next. When all the gel coats have been applied, allow the repair to cure fully before starting to rub down the finished surface. If time allows, it is best to leave the gel coat for several days before carrying out any further work: the harder the gel coat, the easier it will be to obtain a good finish.

A major problem is obtaining a good colour match, even if the same pigment is used, since the percentage added affects the density of the colour. Another drawback is that tiny air bubbles may become trapped in the gel coat, although this can be avoided by applying several thin coats. Despite the difficulties, if the original component is rare or valuable, this may be the only method open to you.

Repairing stress cracks

Another type of repair that may need to be undertaken is not necessitated by damage, but old age. Quite often, older GRP components (car bodies are prime examples) suffer from fine cobweb-like cracks that radiate out from certain areas. With a car, these usually occur around the headlights, windscreen pillars and any openings in the bodywork.

This form of cracking is caused by the release of stress, which builds up within the laminate as it cures when the component is made. During the first few years of the component's life, the laminate continues to harden, but eventually it reaches a turning point, when a small degree of softening takes place. This results in the gel coat cracking, usually in the areas mentioned. Many such components are rectified by sanding down and painting, but this is a very short-term solution because the paint merely bridges the cracks, and it's only a matter of time before they reappear.

Although an old component can never be made as good as new, with a little more effort, a longer lasting repair can be achieved. The first task is to remove the old gel coat with an electric sander. Sand down until the chopped strand matt has been exposed. If the component is small, you could sand the entire surface in this manner, but if it is something large (like a car body), the repair may have to be restricted to the affected areas. In the latter case, sand back as far as practicable from the cracked area.

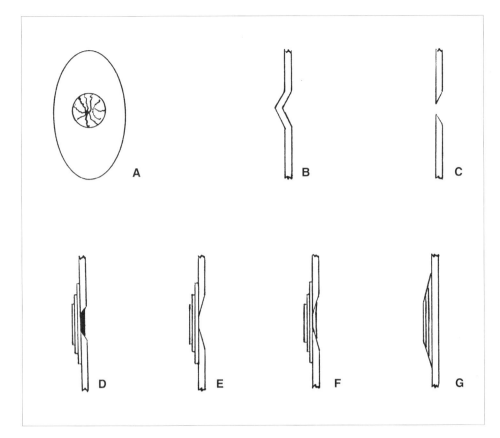

This method can be adapted to make good a variety of damage.
A Point impact damage in a GRP component.
B Section through damage.
C Section through damage after the deformed portion has been sanded off.
D Several plies of chopped strand matt, approximately equal in thickness to the original component, are added across the back of the damaged area. Note the temporary plug in the hole to support the laminate.
E The plug is removed and the area around the repair sanded. Note the tapered edges around the hole.
F A thin lamination is applied to the face side of the damage.
G The repair is completed by filling and sanding.

The next stage is to paint a coat of polyester laminating resin over the exposed chopped strand matt and allow it to cure. If this coat of resin soaks in, apply another when it is almost tack-free. This second coat is unlikely to soak in as well, but if it does, allow it to become almost tack-free and apply yet another. Follow this with a thin layer of gel coat. When this has become tack-free, apply another coat. The smoothness of this second coat will determine whether you need to add a third. Allow the gel coat to cure fully, then use wet-or-dry abrasive paper to rub the repaired area down to the required shape and finish. Finally, prime and paint.

It is possible to self-colour the gel coat, but if the component is old, you are unlikely to be able to match the original colour. However, if you have decided to paint the repaired component, using a pigment in the gel coat will help. Pale grey is a good colour for painting over.

This type of repair can be taken a stage further, although it is not always practical to do so. If you can gain access to the back of the damaged area, sand it down and laminate on two plies of normal chopped strand matt, 450g/sq.m (1½oz/sq.ft) being ideal. Although not essential, this will add a little extra stability to the repaired area.

Most GRP repairs are variations of the methods outlined here. However, for minor damage, such as a dent, begin by sanding down the reverse face to the original contour, even if this means going partially through the laminate. Add a patch to the back, as before, then make good the front by filling. Epoxy laminates can be repaired in the same way. Stress cracks are unlikely to appear on well-made epoxy components, so most epoxy repairs will be necessitated by damage.

Small dents and chipped self-coloured gel coat finishes, etc, are relatively straightforward to repair. The former can be filled with body filler. However, if you want to match a self-coloured gel coat, do not fill the dam-

Facing page

MODIFYING GRP COMPONENTS
These diagrams show the basic
principles involved in modifying
an existing GRP component by
adding another part. An air
scoop or duct is shown, but the
techniques can be used for
making a variety of alterations.
A First, a pattern must be made
and stuck to the component, as
shown in these two views.
B A laminated mould is formed
over the pattern.
C & D The completed mould
after removal from the pattern.
E If the new piece is to be made
in the mould and bonded to the
component as a second stage,
the return flanges of the mould
must be extended by the wall
thickness of the component. If it
is to be laminated directly on to
the component, there is no need
to do this. Instead, the hole for
the duct should be cut out and
the mould stuck in place
temporarily with water-soluble
adhesive or very thin double-
sided adhesive tape. Then the
new piece can be laminated
through the hole. When cutting
the chopped strand matt for
laminating in situ, remember to
allow for it to pass through the
hole and be laminated on to the
underside of the component.
F The scoop in the mould.
G & H Two views of the
laminated scoop.
I A suitable hole is cut in the
existing component.
J The scoop is bonded to the
underside of the component.
Where a modification is not over
a hole in the existing
component, in most cases, it
will be easier to make the new
piece separately, then bond it
on, making good the joint lines
with body filler.

aged area to the original contour, but leave it low enough to allow the application of at least three thin gel coats over the repair. These can be sanded and polished without fear of breaking through the gel coat.

Where only the gel coat has been damaged, no filler will be required. If the damage is recent, it's best to carefully remove any loose particles of gel coat and lift off any pieces that appear cracked, but are still in place. Then simply overfill the chipped area with correctly pigmented gel coat. Allow it to cure fully—remember, the harder the gel coat, the easier it is to obtain a good finish. When repairing newly chipped gel coat, leave the irregular shape of the damaged area as it is, since the repair will be less obvious than when the area has been sanded to a more regular shape. If the damage is an old wound, it will need abrading to achieve a clean surface so that the new gel coat will adhere to it.

When carrying out repairs, matching a self-coloured gel coat will not be easy, but it can be done. Some colours are easier than others to match.

If the repair is to be painted afterwards, all you need do is fill the dent and sand it down to the correct contour. Commercial body fillers usually have good adhesive properties, so simply make sure that the surface to which the filler will be applied is clean.

Modifying existing components

Modifications to GRP components require slightly different techniques to achieve the desired result. If the proposed modification is an extension to the edge of a component, or the addition of a flange of some kind, begin by tapering the edge with an electric sander. Also, sand back through any gel coat for a distance of approximately twice the width of the proposed addition. As the new piece will be added to the edge of the component, both sides of the laminate should be sanded back. Then calculate the number of glass plies needed to make up the component thickness, and laminate half on each side of the prepared area. Ideally, this should be carried out with epoxy laminating resin, but if this is not available, polyester will make an acceptable modification. When working on the edge of a component in this way, some form of support will be required upon which to laminate the glass. Strips of plastic or thin plywood, or even stiff card, stuck in position with blobs of body filler or modelling clay would be suitable. If card or plywood is used, remember that it must be sealed well and waxed to release the laminate. With the modification laminated, all that remains is to apply some gel coat, rub it down and paint to match the original finish.

If a modification is to be made to the surface of a component (for example, the addition of a bulge or external duct), some form of temporary mould will be required to allow the lamination of the part. The latter can either take place off the component, with the new part being bonded on as a second operation, or directly on the component.

When adding an external modification such as a dome or something similar, the new part can be made in a mould, then a hole cut in the component and the part bonded in from the back. Finally, body filler should be used to blend the new part into the old. If you choose to carry out a modification in this way, you will need to make a pattern and a mould, as described in Chapters 3 and 4. Remember that the new part will need a flange around the edge so that it can be bonded in.

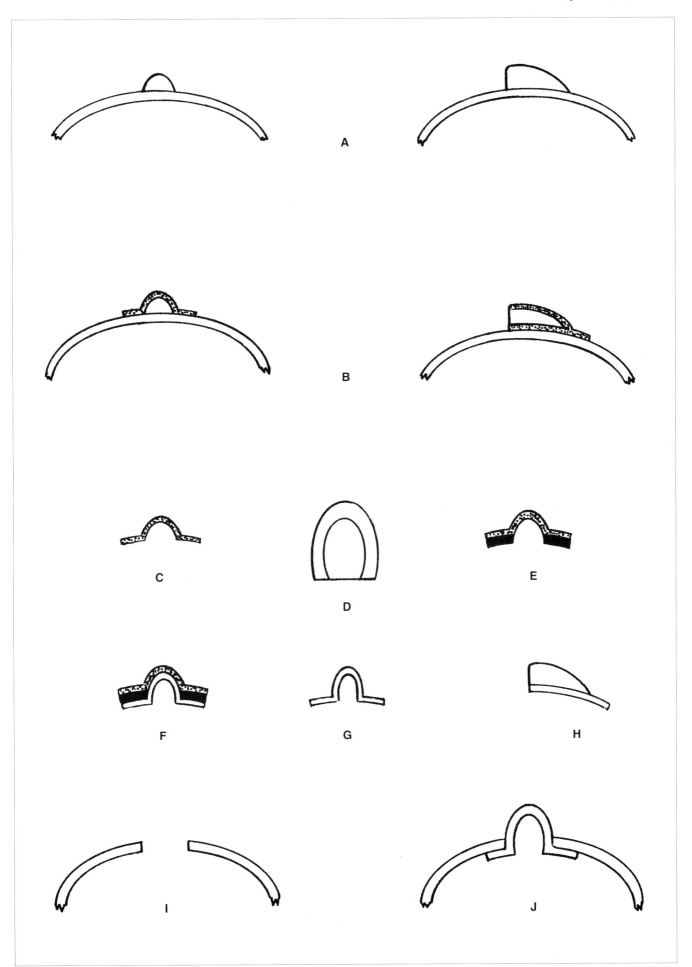

Facing page

EXTENDING GRP COMPONENTS

In some cases, it may be necessary to extend an existing GRP component.

A Section through an existing component requiring an edge modification, such as a vehicle wheel arch.

B A block of suitable pattern material is temporarily attached.

C The pattern material is carved to the required shape.

D A mould is laminated over the finished pattern and surrounding surface.

E The mould after removal from the pattern.

F The mould return flange is extended by the wall thickness of the existing component and the new piece laminated into it.

G The new piece is bonded into position on the original part.

H Alternatively, the mould can be temporarily held to the existing component and the extension laminated in situ.

I Finally, remove the mould.

Alternatively, the new part can be moulded directly on to the component being modified, which is the only solution if there will be no opening through it. Again, a pattern and mould are required. In this case, the most practical move is to make a pattern directly on the component, or make it off the component and stick it in position. The pattern can be made from any suitable material, such as foam, balsa or any other wood, and stuck in position with blobs of body filler or double-sided adhesive tape. The latter method has the advantage that it doesn't do any damage and is easy to remove.

When shaped and blended into the original component, the pattern must be given a thorough release treatment. It is a good idea to apply wax followed by PVA, as this will guarantee release. Also treat the area of the component around the pattern so that the mould can be removed.

The next step is to laminate the mould. As this will only be required temporarily and is likely to have sufficient shape to stiffen it, there is no need to make it very thick: two, or maybe three, plies of 450g/sq.m (1½oz/sq.ft) chopped strand matt would be ideal. Allow it to cure, then remove it with the pattern. Before removing it, however, mark its position carefully so that it can be put back in exactly the same position. Trim the mould if necessary, then apply the release as for any other laminating.

Prepare the component to receive the modification, that is cut any aperture that forms part of the modification or, if there is no cut-out, sand the component over the area to take the new part, removing any paint or gel coat. Sand down to the glass matt and, where there is an aperture, sand around the underside.

When ready to add the new part, first of all gel coat the mould. When it is almost tack-free, laminate the glass matt into place. If the modification will be formed over an aperture in the main component, allow the glass matt to extend beyond the edge of the mould by approximately 25mm (1in). When the laminate is fully wetted out and consolidated, the mould can be put in place, but first the matt that extends beyond the mould should be passed through the aperture in the main component. Stick the mould back in position, using double-sided adhesive tape between the mould flange and component, or strong ordinary tape over the flange. No pressure is needed; the mould simply has to remain in place while the resin sets. When the mould is in position, the wetted glass matt that protrudes through the aperture can be consolidated on to the underside of the component. If the new part is open on one side, but does not sit over an aperture, the wetted out glass that extends beyond the mould should be turned inwards and consolidated down. When the laminate has cured, the mould can be removed, and the modification cleaned up and finished to match the component.

Some modifications may take the form of extensions or swellings to the main component, and the mould may not have an open side through which to laminate. In this situation, the pattern is built up on the component and a mould made in the same manner, but the new part is laminated in the mould and allowed to cure. Then it is removed, trimmed and bonded to the surface of the main component with two-part epoxy adhesive or body filler. The same type of filler can be used to blend the new piece into the original. All that remains is to paint the component to complete the job.

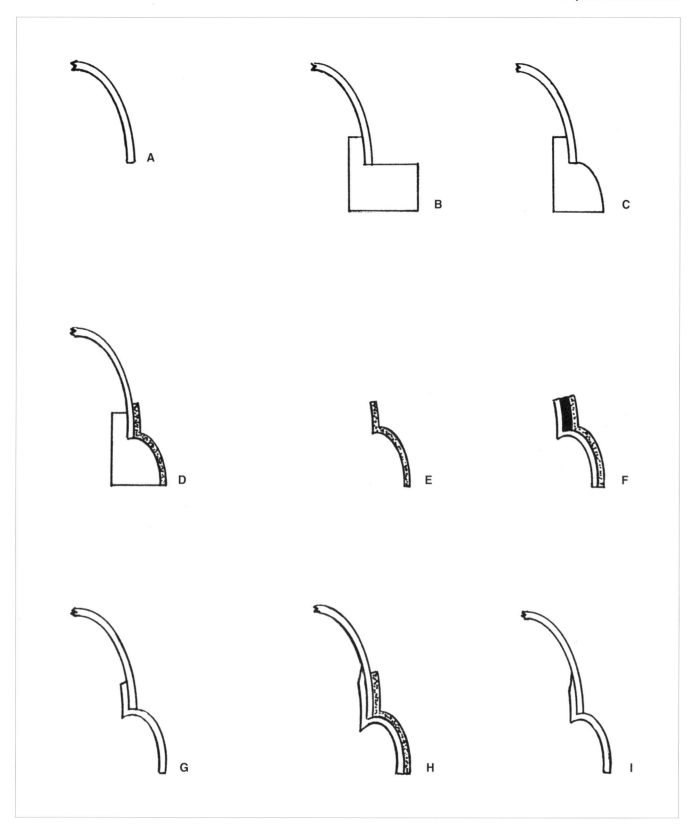

It would be impossible to describe all the many types of GRP repair and modification. Most will be variations of what has been described. In many cases, a specific method may have to be devised for a particular situation, but the same basic principles will apply: that is preparation, materials, laminating and finishing. Remember that the ideal way of doing a job may not always be the most practical, so be prepared to compromise, bearing in mind your abilities, the available materials, facilities, etc.

Troubleshooting

G RP laminating is a craft and, like all crafts, requires skill from the practitioner. However, not even the most experienced laminator is infallible, so there is always the possibility of error. This chapter will describe the most common mistakes and give advice on how to put things right.

The mistake that most laminators will have made at some time or other is to forget to add catalyst to the resin. As a result, the laminate fails to cure. If after seven or eight hours, or more, the resin is still wet, you can be sure that it is uncatalysed. The only remedy is to remove all the laminate while it is still wet. Then wipe out the mould as thoroughly as possible, and immediately laminate the component again. This will absorb the inevitable random fibres left in the mould. Also, the fresh correctly catalysed resin will cure any small amount of resin left on the mould's surface. If an uncatalysed laminate is left for too long, it will tend to dry, but will never cure. If this occurs, the mould will be more difficult to clean out.

Using an insufficient amount of catalyst will result in a partial cure of the laminate. This will tend to be dry, but not hard. It will be flexible, rather like stiff cardboard, and in this state is only fit for scrap. There is no remedy; simply remove the component from the mould, throw it away and begin again.

Blow-outs

Sometimes, when a component is removed from the mould, it will have small faults that can be rectified to save it. One such fault is commonly known as a blow-out. This is a hole caused by air being trapped behind the gel coat when the wetted glass has not been consolidated fully. These normally occur at sharp corners or detail, but may be at any point the roller or brush has missed. All laminators experience blow-outs at some time. If they are not too large, or if there are only a few, the remedy is to break them open and simply fill them slightly proud of the surface with gel coat or, if the component is to be painted, with normal body filler. When the filled areas have cured fully, sand them down to the correct profile. If gel coat has been used, polish the repairs with cutting compound to match the rest of the component; if filler has been employed, prime and paint.

Blisters, wrinkles and depressions

Another fault that occurs from time to time is blistering of the gel coat. There are two main reasons for blisters appearing, although they are connected. If, when the blisters are cut open, the resin underneath is still tacky, the cause is usually inadequate mixing. With polyester resins, the mixing ratio requires a low percentage of catalyst, and if the mixed resin has not been stirred sufficiently, this small amount of catalyst may not come into contact with all of the resin. The result is that some uncatalysed resin will find its way into the lamination and cause the blisters. The other cause of blisters can be insufficient catalyst to activate all of the resin. Of the two, poor mixing is the most common cause of blisters; usually, when there is insufficient catalyst, the laminate is very slow to cure or doesn't cure properly at all.

Sometimes a moulded component may appear to be correct in most aspects, but will have wrinkles in the gel coat. Normally, if the mould has a perfect surface, these wrinkles will be due to the laminating resin remaining in the wet state for too long. The cause can be too little catalyst, or the lamination being carried out in very cold or damp conditions that retard the cure. If the gel coat has a self-coloured finish, the wrinkled areas will need abrading lightly to remove any release agents transferred from the mould. A wire brush will get into the wrinkles quite well. Then slightly overfill the wrinkled areas with gel coat and, when well cured, rub it down and polish it. If the component is to be painted, the wrinkles can be filled with body filler and painted.

Often, on components made with polyester gel coats, the gel coat may appear not to have reached into areas where there are corners or detail. Instead of a sharp corner, there will be a concave depression. This type of fault is caused by an excessive build-up of gel coat in these areas during application, the fault being caused by shrinkage of the gel coat during the cure. As already mentioned, where a thick gel coat is required, it is best applied in more than one coat, which will prevent shrinkage. To rectify the problem of shrinkage, simply overfill the fault with matching gel coat and, when well cured, rub down to the correct contour and polish.

Dry areas

With hand lay-up of polyester components, a fault that occurs quite regularly takes the form of dry areas, that is portions of the laminate that have not been wetted out fully. These usually occur at points that are not in full view at the time of laminating (an overhung area for instance). Moreover, it's very easy to miss an area when wetting out the glass matt. Where there are several plies of glass matt, it is unlikely that a dry area will run through all the plies. However, a dry area may extend to the edge of a component, which will prevent it from being sanded to a clean finish because the under-resinated glass matt will simply fray. This often means that the edge at this point has no stiffness.

To rectify a dry area, sand off the unresinated glass matt, working through as many plies as necessary until you reach a fully resinated base. With a thin laminate, this may mean going as far as the gel coat, so great care will be needed. When the dry glass has been removed, simply laminate some fresh glass matt over the area, taking this new laminate slightly on to the surrounding sound area. Where several plies are involved, make each layer a little larger in area than the previous ply. This will prevent the formation of a steep edge or step to the repaired area.

Dry areas can occur with epoxy laminations when the glass fabric is wetted out in the mould, but are less likely when it is wetted out on the

This swimming pool liner is suffering from a bad case of osmosis—porous areas in the laminate filling with water. GRP boats also suffer from this problem. The main cause is a poorly consolidated laminate with a porous gel coat. Incorrect material choice can also contribute to this problem.

The pool liner was repaired by sanding away all the old gel coat and exposing the unconsolidated areas of the laminate. The entire pool was allowed to dry thoroughly, then it was sealed with fresh resin, as shown here.

The pool after the final stage of repair, the application of a new gel coat. With this type of repair, it is advisable to consult a GRP supplier to ensure that the correct materials are used.

bench, then transferred to the mould. This type of fault is rectified in the same manner as for polyester laminates, except that epoxy resin should be used for the repair.

Pin-holes

A persistent fault found in epoxy components, when no gel coat is used, is the presence of tiny pin-holes in the surface. Although hardly notice-able, they can prove a nuisance when trying to paint the finished compo-nent. These pin-holes will not always be present, especially when the lam-inate is only one or two plies thick and the cure has been carried out under vacuum. This is because, with a thin lay-up, the vacuum pump can pull most of the trapped air through the glass fabric and out of the laminate.

If an epoxy component does display this type of surface porosity, the best remedy is to use a primer/filler paint. Apply a thin coat and rub it down, then repeat the process. This should have filled all the tiny holes. If not, prime again before applying the desired paint finish. Attempting to fill the pin-holes with epoxy resin and painting over them, doesn't work very well; surface tension appears to prevent the resin from getting into the very tiny holes.

It would be very difficult to list all the possible faults that may be found at some time or other when utilizing GRP technology. This chapter has cov-ered the most common problems, although you may come across others. However, in many cases, these will be variants of those described. Once some GRP work has been carried out and experience gained, finding the causes of faults will become much easier, as will determining suitable methods of rectification.

14

Resin casting

Although resin casting is not a true GRP technique, as there is no glass involved (with the exception that sometimes glass flakes are mixed into the resin to add strength), nevertheless it is a technology that has a lot to offer. It is a very interesting, yet simple, process that can result in excellent components, and can be taken advantage of by anyone with the minimum of equipment. Resin casting is employed in the manufacture of a wide range of items, including statues, models, plaques, badges and detailed finishing pieces for a wide range of applications, such as furniture, architecture and any other situations where detailing would be difficult to mould or carve.

As with GRP moulding, the process begins with a pattern and, as the mould will be formed from self-releasing silicone rubber, this pattern can be made from almost any material. The mould can be taken from an existing item (a badge or plaque for example), and because the rubber is so flexible, the surface of the pattern does not need any special preparation. In fact, the rubber will release from almost any surface texture, and that includes undercuts. Silicone rubber moulding materials can be bought from all GRP suppliers and many model stores.

There are two basic methods of making the rubber mould. One is to coat the pattern with the liquid rubber which, when cured, can simply be peeled off. This technique is utilized for statues and models. Alternatively, the pattern can be placed in a shallow box or tray and the liquid poured over it, resulting in a more solid rubber mould. This method is employed for plaques, badges and any flat, or nearly flat, items. Instructions for mixing and using moulding rubbers will be supplied by the manufacturer.

Making castings

The casting resin can be polyester or epoxy. For most decorative and similar applications, the former is used; epoxy tends to be chosen for more technical purposes, such as potting and encapsulating electronic components. Polyester casting resins will require a catalyst, while epoxy systems will be two-part mixes, the same as for laminating.

The process is quite straightforward: it is simply a matter of mixing the resin and pouring it into the mould. However, the most common problem with resin casting is the entrapment of air, which results in blow-holes in the finished item. Various methods can be used to reduce the likelihood of this problem occurring.

If a vacuum pump is available, it can be utilized in one of two ways, but only with an epoxy casting resin. One method is to put the mixed resin into a sturdy vessel of some type and pull vacuum in the vessel to remove any air that has been mixed in. Then pour the resin slowly into the mould, down one side where possible, since this allows air to escape as the resin flows in. The other method is to put the mould containing the resin into the vessel and apply vacuum, although this is not likely to be totally successful with a deep mould. Epoxy casting resins have a long pot life to allow time for any air to come to the surface.

A simple means of making a suitable vacuum vessel is to use a length of thick-walled steel pipe. This can be closed off at top and bottom by aluminium plates with sheets of rubber to form gaskets. There is no need to fix the plates to the pipe, as the vacuum will hold them firmly in place. You simply stand the pipe on the base plate with the rubber sheet between them, then put the mould or pot of mixed resin inside the pipe. Place the second rubber sheet over the pipe, followed by the top plate, which should be fitted with a connector for the vacuum pipe. Finally, turn on the vacuum pump. If the resin filled mould has been placed in the vessel, the time it spends under vacuum will not be limited, but if a pot of mixed resin is being treated, remember that it must still be poured into the mould.

As mentioned elsewhere, polyester resins should not be cured under vacuum, as this tends to pull out the styrene, which can adversely affect the cure. However, polyester casting resin is an excellent material that works well and is simple to use.

As with epoxy resins, polyesters can be modified to provide a wide range of different finishes to the item being cast. As well as an endless range of colours, there are textured additives that represent stone, marble, slate and many other materials. Metallic powders can also be added so that the surface of the cast item can be buffed with an electric polisher to produce a finish that resembles metal. For example, when bronze powder is used and the finished item polished, it looks exactly like real bronze. When this technique is used on a statue, the high spots polish up to a bright finish, leaving the crevices and deep detail dark. The result is an antique look.

When the casting is shallow, like a plaque, most of the air will float to the surface, and since this will be the back of the item, any resulting bubbles will not matter. It is a good idea to tap the pot of mixed resin rapidly on the bench before pouring, as this will help bring any air to the top of the mix. Allow this to disperse before pouring the resin slowly into the mould. If this has an open shallow shape, pour the resin in at one side or end, and allow it to flow over the detail by its own self-levelling nature until the mould is full. If the mould is of a deep shape (a statue or something similar), tilt the mould and slowly pour the resin down the lower side. This ensures that the resin reaches the bottom of the mould on one side first, thus pushing the air out as the mould fills up. In almost all cases, deep moulds like this will be of the thin-walled flexible type, and it is a good idea to gently squeeze the mould as the resin is poured in. This will dislodge air from the deeper parts of the detail and undercut areas, where normally it would be trapped.

A thin very flexible mould will need supporting when filled with resin. One method is to make a case to fit around the outside of the mould. A variety of materials can be used: for example, plaster of Paris, modelling

A pattern for a cast resin crest.

The rubber mould taken from the pattern.

The casting resin still in the mould. Note the shrinkage of the resin around the edges.

The cast resin crest removed
from the mould.

Below A close-up of the finished
cast resin crest.

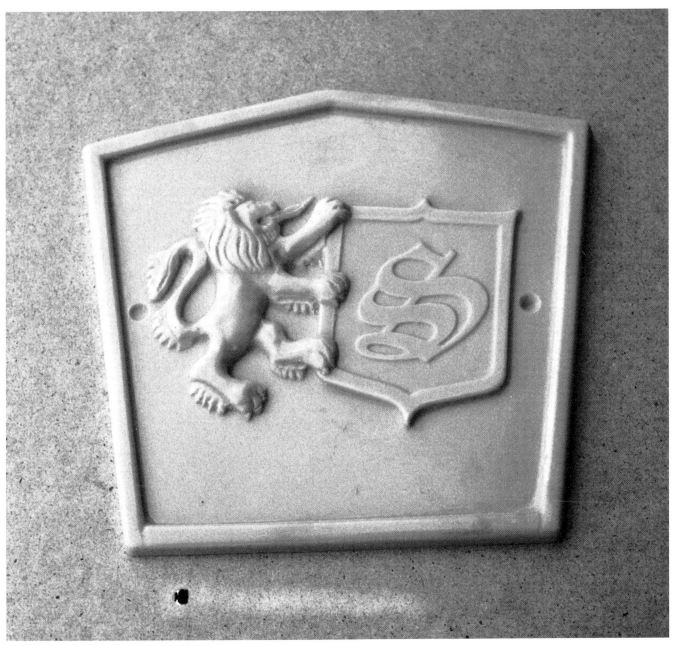

This resin figurine was cast in two parts, the hand being coloured to represent marble and the base to resemble rock.

The mould in which the figurine was cast. It is made of rubber, but has a GRP outer shell to keep it in shape.

clay or papier mâché. The case should be cut through the centre with a fine saw, into two or more pieces, then it can be assembled around the filled mould and held together with rubber bands. Some moulds of this type can simply be hung in some form of frame. An easy way of doing this is to cut a hole in a cardboard box and hang the mould through the hole.

When the resin has cured, the casting can be removed from the mould. With an open type of mould, you should gently lever the item out, taking care not to damage the rubber. A thin flexible mould can be peeled off the item. In some cases, it will be possible to roll the mould off the casting, then unroll it to make another. A great advantage of rubber moulds is that they require no release agent or other preparation before use.

When the casting has been removed from the mould, very little is left to do, as the mould will produce the desired type of detail and finish. All that remains is to level off the bottom or reverse face of the casting, by sanding it (rubbing the casting over a sheet of abrasive paper laid on a flat surface works well), and fix it to a mount, facia, etc. In the case of a statue, it may have a piece of baize glued to its base. Some items may need casting in more than one piece, in which case, the pieces will need gluing together; two-part epoxy adhesive is ideal for this.

This chapter is intended as a guide to the potential of resin casting, which is a technique without hard and fast rules. Consequently, you can develop methods and uses to meet your own needs. As casting resins can vary so much from one manufacturer to another, you should consult the supplier, who will help you select the best materials for the job and provide information on how to use them, together with the relevant safety data.

Resin casting can be used to produce a wide range of items. The technique can be taken advantage of by almost anyone. It requires a minimum of equipment and little space in which to work. As a result, it is equally suitable as the basis for an enjoyable pastime or a serious business.

Two more examples of cast resin figurines.

15

Health & safety

Any person with the ability to take advantage of the skills and techniques outlined in the previous chapters should be aware of the need for his or her own safety, and take the necessary steps to understand the materials and processes involved. Since this book does not describe the use of specific branded products, it is not possible to give precise safety instructions here. This information will depend upon the chemical formulations used by the manufacturers of the materials being employed. Consequently, the user must obtain and read the relevant technique and safety data sheets for the materials that have been chosen. These will provide detailed processing instructions and health and safety considerations. It is essential that this information is obtained when the materials are purchased and acted on when they are being processed.

Safety data sheets are available for all products used in GRP laminating, but the amount of information they contain will vary from one to another. This is because there will be more safety considerations with hazardous materials than non-hazardous products. Much of the information the sheets do provide, and the way in which it is presented, is controlled by regulation.

Listing the hazards

In general, a safety data sheet will provide a description of the product, giving its physical and chemical properties, among which will be its appearance, smell and such information as the flash point, boiling point and whether or not it is soluble in water. The sheet will go on to set out the hazards, if any, that the product presents. For example, polyester resin may be described as a harmful, flammable marine pollutant with an irritant vapour, while the solvent acetone (used for cleaning brushes and equipment) will be listed as a highly flammable, explosive irritant that produces narcotic vapours. PVA release agent, on the other hand, is likely to be described as non-hazardous and non-toxic.

Most of the materials used in GRP work can produce harmful side effects, and the relevant safety data sheet will list the physical responses and symptoms of over-exposure to each product, together with the appropriate medical action that should be taken. The various resins, for example, can cause severe irritation if allowed to come into contact with the skin or eyes (phenolic resins can actually produce burns), while inhalation of the fumes they give off may, in severe cases, cause unconciousness. Needless to say, users of these materials should not eat or drink while working, in case of accidental ingestion, which could cause internal injuries. The safety data sheet will give advice for the provision of immediate first aid to deal with any problems that are likely to occur and, invariably, will specify that professional medical assistance should be sought as soon as possible.

Since many of the materials used in GRP work are flammable, methods of fighting the fires they may cause feature prominently on the data sheets. The types of fire extinguishers required will be specified, as will any special precautions that should be taken by fire fighters, such as wearing breathing apparatus and keeping containers of the product cool by spraying them with water. Of course, no one should smoke while carrying out GRP work or when in the vicinity of such work.

The safe storage of GRP materials is also paramount because of their hazardous nature, and the data sheet will set out the suitable conditions for this. Polyester resins, for example, should be stored in a dry, well ventilated place, away from any form of ignition or heat and at a temperature below 25°C (77°F). They should be kept away from peroxides, which form the basis of many catalysts. Other materials will have similar specific requirements.

In addition, information will be given on many other pertinent subjects, including stability and reactivity, transportation, handling, toxicology, environmental considerations, safe disposal, whether protective clothing should be worn and, if so, what that clothing should comprise.

Safety data sheets are even available for products that are not liquid chemical formulations, such as chopped strand matt. In fact, the information on this solid dry material is likely to be quite extensive. Although this will probably include a statement to the effect that there are no known carcinogenic hazards, the product may be listed as an irritant, both through inhalation and skin or eye contact.

At first glance, the data sheets for many of the materials used in GRP laminating would make them appear hazardous and, if they are not used with care, that is indeed the case. However, the purpose of those data sheets is to make the user aware of the possible hazards and provide the necessary information to allow their safe use.

Common sense

When using these types of material, safety is often a matter of common sense. The GRP process has been employed by many people for a very long time, and they range from individuals making one-off products in home workshops to those running very successful GRP manufacturing businesses. As can be imagined, the conditions under which this work is carried out vary from the most basic to the ideal, but serious injury or damage to health is rarely caused.

Although all the safety data sheets warn of the possible hazards and how to guard against them, whenever this type of work is being carried out, there is one simple precaution that should become second nature, and that is to wear protective clothing when carrying out any form of GRP work. Overalls, preferably the disposable type, are a must, as are impervious gloves. When necessary, protective footwear, protective spectacles or goggles and dust/vapour masks should also be worn. Remember, when working with GRP, your safety is in your own hands.

Conclusion

It would be impossible for a book of this type to cover every method and technique used in GRP manufacture, as there are no set rules governing how jobs should be done. Almost all users will develop methods that suit their particular needs and the equipment, or lack of it, at their disposal. Consequently, the text has been written to give as broad a description as possible of the basic methods and techniques that are employed.

The materials used in GRP technology have also been described, together with their suitable applications. However, there will be variants of these, with specifications designed to meet particular requirements. Therefore, it is always sensible to consult the nearest supplier, who will advise on the best material for the job in hand.

GRP technology has a lot to offer, and its use is open to anyone who wants to take advantage of its great potential. Just how much can be achieved, however, will depend entirely on how determined the potential user is to learn.

Index

A
Abrasive paper 9
Abrasive plane 10
Accelerator 13, 71
Acetone 32
Aerosil 14
Air bleed layer 78-79
Aircraft parts, non-structural 12
Aluminium powder 14
Ambient-temperature cure 40, 44
Autoclave 13
Automotive applications 12

B
Balsa wood, as core material 19
Boat applications 12
Brass powder 14
Bronze powder 14
Brushes 8
Building partitions 19

C
Carbon fibre fabrics 85
Catalyst 12, 15, 71
  activity level 12, 61
  measure 9, 30
  mixing ratio 29-30, 62
    chart 30
  choice of 12
Caul plate 100-101
China clay 14, 25
Chopped strand matt 16
  binder 16
Closed-mould laminating 94-101
  pattern 97
  pressure pot 95, 97
  process time 97
  resin for 100
  resin flow 94
  special glass matts 94
  vacuum transfer of resin 97-101
Colouring paste 13, 28-29
Components
  attaching metal brackets and inserts 70
  final detailing 70-71, 85
  removal from mould 66-70, 85
  removing mould joint lines 70
Consolidating rollers 8
Continuous glass rovings 17
Copper powder 14
Core materials 18-19, 102-105
Core matt 19

  use of 51
Craft knife 9
Crush resistance, of hollow components 17
Cutting polish 15
Cutting templates 58-60, 76

D
Dealing with tight corners, when making moulds 34-36
Double-sided mould 16
Draught angle 26, 27
Dust masks 10

E
Electric drill 10
Electric sander 10
Epoxy laminating 74-85
  finishing components 85
  methods of wetting out 77-78
  moulds for 74
  preparing laminate for vacuum pressure 78-82
  release agents 74
  resin-to-glass ratio 77-78
Epoxy resin systems 13
  core materials 19
  cure cycle 13, 74
  equipment required 10
  gel coats 74-75
  hardener 76
  mixing 76
  pot life 76
  suitable reinforcement 75-76
Exotherm 13, 32, 64, 92
Expansion resistance, of hollow components 17

F
Filament winding 17
Filler paste 14
Fire-retardant materials 14
First aid kit 10
Foams 18-19
  as core materials 102-105
  barrier layer 102
  glueing 102, 103
  phenolic 102-103
  polystyrene 19, 102
  polyurethane 18, 102
  PVC 19, 102
  shaping 104
  two-part liquid 102, 105

G
G-cramps 10
Gel coats
  applying 8, 9, 32, 56
  general-purpose 12
  measuring thickness 29
  pigmenting 28-29
  pot life 30
  pre-mixed 13
  range of 12
  self-coloured finish 8, 30
    application of 56-58
  shrinkage of 29
  voids in 29
General applications 12
Glass-fibre tapes 18
Glass flakes 18
Glass reinforcements 16-18
Glass tissue 16

H
Hand cleaner 10
Hand drill 10
Health and safety 124
Honeycomb core materials 19, 104
  for use with epoxy resin systems 19
Hoop strength 17
Hot-melt glue gun 22
Hot-wire cutter 102, 104

I
Interlaminar strength 17, 56, 74, 75
Iron powder 14

K
Kevlar fabrics 85

L
Laminate
  avoiding voids in 37
  balancing fibres in 18
  putting down multi-plies 39
  thickness 50-56
Large panels 18, 19, 51
Liquid sealers 15

M
Marble powder 14
Matched-mould laminating 90-91
Materials 12-19
  choosing 50
Metal mould 15
Metallic powders 119

Mixing vessels 8
Modelling clay 14
Modifications to GRP components
  111-113
Mohair roller 9
Moulds
  adding surface tissue 33
  additions to 48
  building up the lamination 37-40
  component removal 66-70
  deciding on thickness 38-40
  making 28-49
  male 65
  matched 90-91
  materials 14, 16
  preparing for use 45-49
  quality 20
  release coating 45, 48
  removing from pattern 44-45
    use of compressed air 44-45
  repairing defects 49
  types 23
Multi-section moulds 10, 21, 23, 27, 35
  clamp bolt size and spacing 44
  component removal 66-69
  locating devices 41-43
  making 41-44
  mating flange width 44
  gel coating 32
  sealing joints 45

O
Overalls 10

P
Paper rope 19
Patterns
  attaching weirs 21, 27
  base boards 23-24
  bracing 20-21
  creating, from scratch 24-26
    from existing components 20-21
    from blocks 25
    from formers 25
  making 15, 16, 20-27
  materials 20, 24-25
  release coating 27
  release failure 27
  shaping and finishing 26-27
  solid 24-25
  surfacers 20
Peel ply 85
Phenolic laminating 86-89
  release agents 86
Phenolic resins 86
  gel coats 86-87
  hardeners 87-88
  post cure 88-89
  processing techniques 87
  reinforcement 88
  surface finish 89
  use of 86
Pipes, production of 17

Plasticene 14
Polyester laminating 17, 50-73
  cure 66
Polyester resin 12, 13, 14
  calculating amount required 33-34, 60
  mixing ratio 33, 60
  pot life 61
Poly vinyl alcohol, see PVA
Positive-pressure laminating 90-91
Post cure 40-41, 44, 88-89
Power filler 25
Pressure vessels, production of 17
Protective clothing 11
Protective spectacles 10
PVA 15, 27
  removing 41

R
Release agents 15
  aerosol 15
  applying 27, 45, 48, 50
  chemical 15
  enhanced temperature resistance 15
  liquid versions 15, 50
  modified 12
  PVA 15
  wax 15
Release membrane 78
Repairs to GRP components 106-111
Resin casting 118-123
  blow-holes 118
  moulds 118
    releasing castings from 123
    supporting 119-123
  patterns for 118
  processing techniques 118-123
Resins 12-14
  additives 14
  calculating amount required 60
  casting 14
  epoxy 13
  fire-retardant properties 12
  flow coating 13, 14
  general-purpose polyester 12
  important considerations 50
  improved heat resistance 12
  modified 12
  polyester 12, 13
  pot life 61
  top coating 13, 14
Resin-transfer moulding, see Closed-
  mould laminating
Rubber gloves 10
Rubber mallet 10
Rubber moulds 15

S
Sandwich structures 18, 51-55, 102-104
Silicone moulding compounds 15
Silicone rubber, two-part pourable 14
Slate powder 14
Spanners 10
Spatulas 8

Spray laminating 17, 92-93
  mould preparation 92
  consolidation of laminate 92
Stiffening ribs 41
  suitable materials 41
Stippling action 34
Styrene 14
Surface faults, prevention of 16
Surface filler 25
Surform 10
Synthetic tooling blanks 24

T
Talc 14, 25
Temperature controlled oven, see
  Autoclave
Tools and equipment 8-11
Trimming laminates 10
Troubleshooting 114-117
  blow-outs 114
  blisters 114-115
  depressions 115
  dry areas 115
  pin-holes 117
  wrinkles 115
Tubes, production of 17
Two-part moulds 94
  mould seal 94

U
Ultra-violet-resistant compounds 14
Undercuts 26, 28
Unidirectional fibres 18

V
Vacuum bags 74, 79-85, 91, 100-101,
  102
  checking for leaks 83
  forming 79-80
    from rubber 84
  material 79
  rubber 84-85
    sealing 84
  sealing tape 79
  vacuum outlet 80-82
Vacuum cure 13, 82-84
  checking state of cure 83
  cure time 83
  testing vacuum 82
Vacuum gauge 83
Vacuum pump 13, 74, 79, 99, 118
Vinylester resins 13, 71-73

W
Wax 14
  extruded shapes 16
  flat sheets 15, 16
  pattern makers' 84, 90
Weirs 21-23, 28
  attaching 22-23, 27
  materials 21
Woven glass-fibre fabrics 13, 17, 18
Woven rovings 17